Protection With Grace

Keep Your House of Worship Safe

Richard Fletcher

Copyright © 2025 Richard Fletcher
All rights reserved.
ISBN 979-8-89965-777-1

ACKNOWLEDGMENTS

I want to thank Dr. Matt Teis of Liberty Baptist Church in Las Vegas for being a good friend and a strong, compassionate Man of God. Over the years, we have collaborated on various community events, law enforcement initiatives, special projects, and, sadly, law enforcement funerals.

Thank you to my editor, Dr. Eduardo Jesús Arismendi-Pardi, Professor Emeritus of Mathematics (Ret.) at Orange Coast College (1991-2021). Dr. Arismendi-Pardi is also a Revelation Theologian and Liberation Theologian and the author of fifteen mathematics textbooks and various publications in mathematics education, ethnomathematics, applied statistics, liberation theology, and revelation theology. A good friend and neighbor who encouraged me to clarify details and provided feedback in a way that motivated me to write even more. I sometimes felt like I was back in school after reading his edits and 'suggestions.'

Thank you to my family. I have been blessed with such good people. They have been supportive and gently pushed me by asking, "How is the booking coming along?"

To my wonderful wife, Kim. After thirty-four years of marriage, she still supports my crazy ideas. I love you.

And to the Good Lord, Jesus Christ. The grace and mercy shown to me could be its own book.

FORWARD

Liberty Baptist Church of Las Vegas ministered in the most violent area of the city of Las Vegas, according to the Las Vegas Metropolitan Police Department. Their data demonstrated the high violent crime rate and inability to address the needs of these social issues, at the forefront of their intent to adopt a broader approach to policing. They collaborated with the church to initiate Heroes United in the fall of 2013. This partnership enlisted the help of multiple community stakeholders and achieved great success. Violent crime dropped by 75%! Calls for service fell by 27%. It was during this project, I met Richard Fletcher. His first impression as a former Marine, with white hair and a neatly groomed mustache, left the impression of a man who knew his stuff.

In the weeks and months to follow, we partnered together to embrace this community. We tried several programs that found great success, and other initiatives that did not. In each interaction, Rich exuded care for our members, their safety, and future success. We became friends. I learned he is more than an incredible civic servant, but is also a passionate follower of Jesus Christ. He leads a small group for his church and is a model husband to his wife, Kim. He cares deeply about the health of the church and loves America.

When mass shootings shook the headlines across the cultural landscape, he snapped to attention. As the leader of the bureau's honor guard, he knows too well the pain of losing loved ones and the grief associated with these tragedies. Churches' constituents pass through metal detectors and security protocols to visit the weekly worship service. Some lean upon Providence to secure their facilities.

Rich understands church culture and police tactics. He marries these two insights into this volume. Church leaders should embrace the practical tools and insights from his experience, and as good shepherds, protect their flock. Solomon offered sage advice on this subject. He said, *"For by wise counsel thou shalt make thy war: and in multitude of counsellors there is safety."* (Proverbs 24:6, King James Version)

Rich's book will fill a pressing need for the American church leader to equip his ministers to do the Lord's work and walk in the Lord's wisdom. I believe this book will challenge and enhance any church ministry. I am honored to recommend it and Rich to you with full enthusiasm!

> Dr. Matthew Teis
> Executive Pastor
> Liberty Baptist Church of Las Vegas

INTRODUCTION

In the summer of 2022, my Pastor texted me and asked if I wanted to meet for coffee. I agreed, and as soon as I hung up, I told my wife, Kim, that the Pastor would ask me to set up a security team for our small church. She quickly agreed and wished me luck.

And just as my wife and I thought, during the meeting with the Pastor, he asked if I would help set up a team and protocols to help protect the congregation. The pastor was aware of my 25-year work history in law enforcement. He was familiar with some of the programs I had created while serving my community. I agreed, and the only thing I asked for in return was the ability to hear the message every Sunday. I did not want to take a position and not get fed the *Word*. He installed a TV in the foyer so that others and I could watch and receive the message.

On my very first Sunday as the official Security Director — and the only one on the team so far — I saw a residentially challenged man come in. He wanted coffee. I poured him a cup and started to have a conversation with him. Something was off about him; my experience told me things could go south in a split second.

My intuition was correct, as he began asking questions about the various rooms and focused on locating the kids' room. It wasn't hard to determine, as each door was marked, and when he saw the sign for the little kids' room, he immediately started walking briskly to it. I was able to stop him, remove him from the premises, take his photo, and trespass on him without any of the Congregation knowing about it. Thank you, Lord.

Only afterward, when I submitted my report, did the Pastor know what had happened. He recognized the residentially challenged man as being a regular at the church. He was concerned about the person being unable to return for food, coffee, clothes, etc. I told the Pastor the man could come back and we would feed him, but he was not allowed in the building. I finished the conversation by telling the Pastor that it is possible to have *protection with grace*. Protection and grace are distinct concepts but can be understood and implemented together. The Apostle Paul warned us that the wolves would come to the church and try to devour it. People need protection. Only God can give us grace for salvation. Yet, we can still show mercy to those who attempt to steal our possessions or harm us to a certain extent. Zechariah 7:9 states, *"This is what the Lord says; Almighty said: Administer true justice, show mercy and compassion to one another."*

A security team must understand that they protect the congregation, and the church must offer grace and mercy. Security should always treat people with compassion and respect. Yes, it is a balancing act, but I genuinely believe that we are staying in line with biblical teachings by doing so.

That first Sunday, I realized that even with my experience in law enforcement, there was a difference when dealing with church security issues. I looked online at different sources and bought a few books, but I felt something was missing, and I wasn't quite sure what that was, nor could I define it.

That is why, with prayer and my wife's go-ahead, I started writing this book. Houses of Worship of all sizes will find helpful, real-life suggestions and common-sense approaches, and implement protocols they might not have thought of before. I hope to find something to further protect my church and its members while passing along the information.

THE PURPOSE OF THIS BOOK

The primary purpose of this book and the corresponding website, www.protectionwithgrace.com, is to provide resources and information for established or new churches to either improve their existing security measures or establish security protocols to protect the Congregation from a litany of potential threats or medical episodes [issues or dilemmas?]. It is my hope that church leaders will consider this book a comprehensive guide to determining the best practices for their unique church setting while developing a security plan.

Churches need to have a deeper understanding of security and not shy away from the risks and threats they may face. Knowing what they may be, church leaders are better positioned to provide solutions to these risks and threats. Understanding basic security measures to protect the Congregation, prevent theft, create emergency response plans, limit cybersecurity threats, or address medical issues will go a long way in protecting the flock.

Ultimately, I hope that this book helps churches create an environment that is both safe and welcoming for long-time members, guests, and staff. Having the right plans, people, and mindset in place for church security and/or operations is the right thing to do. I intend to provide accurate information based on relevant experience to have prepared churches.

This book and its associated website are dedicated to empowering new and established places of worship. Both aim to provide a complete understanding of the vital need for security and offer confident guidance on knowledge, consultation, design, and implementation of robust security protocols. The wealth of information contained within will serve as an authoritative blueprint for creating best practices and strategic security measures tailored specifically to the unique requirements of your place of worship.

You will be shown different scenarios and solutions to various risks and threats you may face. By the time you have finished this book, you will have a better understanding of how to handle a myriad of situations, from the medical episode to the disruptive person, to the crime in progress, to cybersecurity, and to legal and ethical decisions.

This book is designed to help you confidently establish a safe and secure place of worship for your staff, volunteers, and visitors.

CONTENTS

1	**Liability and concerns**	1
	Growing concerns	3
	Congregations must be protected	4
	Reality of our times	5
	Should churches have security	6
	How does the Bible define security?	7
	What is the role of the church in maintaining security?	8
	Does having a security team make a church feel less welcoming?	8
	Church security protection with grace	10
2	**Organizing church security**	13
	The decision to have security	15
	The need to understand security	17
	A church security survey	19
	Form Letter	23
3	**Roles and Responsibilities**	24
	What is the responsibility of the church security?	24
	Priorities for the safety and well-being of the congregants?	25
	Roles	28

	The ideal security team member	32
	What are the duties of church security?	35
	Should security be identifiable?	36

4	**Communication**	42
	The power of speaking with one voice	42
	Identify a spokesperson for the church during emergencies	43
	Security communication	44
	Write emergency scripts for the Pastoral Team	45
	Different church security teams communicating with each other	48

5	**First responders and the law**	51
	It is not your security team's job to be the police	51
	Should churches work with first responders?	53
	Ask the police to conduct walkthroughs of your church	57
	When to call 9-1-1 or 3-1-1	58
	What should security do when the first responders arrive?	59
	Talk with your LEO congregation	61
	State laws and links	66
	Insurance implications of carrying concealed	70
	What is your position on firearms inside the church?	74

6	**Protocols**	78
	Importance of written protocols for church security	78

Writing reports	80
Maintaining documentation	82
Stop-gap measures for protecting vital information	82
Should your church have a policy about documenting incidents?	84
Why should churches have cash management controls?	86
How can a small church ensure continuity of business?	89

7 Incidents — 91

How do you handle a disruptive church member/visitor?	91
What God's Word says about the use of force.	97
Sometimes, security has to put their hands on people	98
Active Shooter	102
De-brief all incidents	106
Be a good witness	107

8 Common security issues — 108

Three common issues we should not overlook	108
Cybercrimes	111
Who has the passwords?	112
Other considerations	113
Protection measures for tithing and offerings	114
Accidents	119
Events	120
Waivers for trips and events	121

	Victimizations	126
	Child Abuse	126
	Elder Abuse	131
	Adult Sexual Abuse	133
	Spousal Abuse	134
	Signs of an Abuser	140
9	**Facilities**	143
	Access to facilities	144
	Sharing a building	146
	Cameras and installation topics	149
	Electric control panels	154
	Storage of hazardous materials	155
	Unattended bags or boxes left in the church	159
	Medical kits in churches	162
	Fire extinguishers	165
	The building is used as an emergency shelter for the public	166
	Feeding and ministering to the residentially challenged	168
10	**Comments from the survey**	171
	Comments and responses from the nationwide survey	171
11	**Conclusion**	176

Chapter One
Liability and Concerns

"You attract what you present."
Jim, a church member

Liability and Concerns
I spoke with a Pastor and asked what type of attention, or how much, was given in seminary to covering the topic of security in places of worship. The answer was brief and concise – "None." I was told the emphasis is on theology, which makes sense. The basis of theological education is to prepare a seminarian to lead and guide a congregation. Theological curriculum may include budgets, marketing, and human resources, depending on the type of seminary and specialization focus. What does not make sense is why the thought of having a good security team is not on the same level of importance as having a solid budget or ensuring the building looks presentable.

Having a reliable security team is not the same as having budgeting or facilities. Security in places of worship is often an afterthought or is created solely to appease insurance companies. Analysis of the survey data collected for this book revealed that the majority of places of worship lack paid security teams and provide minimal training.

In reality, most security teams are created from existing members and are given minimal direction or training.
We are aware that the security landscape has undergone rapid changes in the last few years.

This also applies to places of worship. One of the significant changes to modern-day security issues is the rise of mass shootings and violent acts in areas that are considered soft targets. churches must be prepared to address these incidents. The mindset of *"It will never happen here"* has not provided compelling evidence that an act of violence resulting in injury or death would ever occur in a place of worship. Security is more than just dealing with criminal activities. Security protocols must be in place to minimize injuries, respond to medical issues, or address natural disasters and other unexpected events.

Assigning an inexperienced person to the parking lot to *handle things* is not an effective security practice. Handing a radio to the same person without proper training should not occur unless written procedures and protocols are in place. Based on the analysis of the *Protection With Grace* survey, there is evidence that churches are addressing security concerns ineffectively by assigning the security issues to a member of the congregation who does not have the proper training and lacks access to a set of policies or procedures contained in a church document that focuses on safety.

Setting up a properly trained security team is the most effective way to address security issues that can result in irreparable damage, injury, or death. The problems resulting from setting up an untrained and inexperienced security system will likely lead to litigation and liability if a person is injured or harmed, thus exposing the church and its leadership to vicarious liability.

Vicarious liability means that if a security member wrongfully harms or kills someone, the clergy person who assigned that person to oversee security concerns is equally responsible and liable. No amount of explanation can exempt the church or its leadership from liability.

The argument that the security member did not follow directions or acted on his own, neither exempts the leaders from liability, nor resolves the issue. As always, the church and its administrative staff are responsible for being knowledgeable of local regulations, policies, and laws governing the city where the church is located. Hence, speaking with the organization's legal representatives to minimize liability issues is advisable.
The church should be aware of and comply with local and state regulations and laws. Legal consultation is advisable for these matters.

Many overlook the importance of having or not having a security team when considering security measures. Typically, security is associated with handling incidents or accidents. However, how your team responds to confrontational or even violent individuals can significantly impact you. Therefore, when establishing a security team, it's crucial to seek out the best candidates and provide them with training based on recommendations from the church's lawyers, insurance representatives, and local law enforcement agencies.

Growing Concerns
Church security is a growing concern in the USA due to the increasing number of violent incidents and attacks on religious institutions. churches are often perceived as easy targets for criminals and extremists, leaving them vulnerable to theft, vandalism, and even mass shootings. Improving security measures, such as installing access control systems, training staff and volunteers, and collaborating with law enforcement, protects the physical safety of church members and visitors and helps maintain the peaceful and welcoming environment that churches aim to provide. This ensures that congregants feel both physically and emotionally secure.

The security landscape has undergone significant changes in recent years, with important implications for churches and other Houses of Worship.

One major change is the increase in mass shootings and other violent attacks on soft targets, such as religious institutions. These attacks have become more frequent and deadlier, leading to a growing awareness of the need for enhanced security measures to protect against these types of threats. churches must be prepared to respond to various potential security incidents, including active shooter scenarios, bomb threats, and other forms of violence.

Another significant change in the security landscape is the growing importance of cybersecurity. As churches and other religious organizations increasingly rely on technology to communicate and manage their operations, they are also becoming more vulnerable to cyberattacks. Hackers may seek to steal sensitive information, disrupt church operations, or spread misinformation or propaganda. churches must be prepared to protect their data and systems from these threats and to develop appropriate cybersecurity policies and procedures to ensure that they are prepared for any potential attacks.

Congregations must be protected.
While the Bible does not explicitly address the issue of church security, it does encourage Christians to take steps to protect themselves and others from harm. For example, the Bible teaches that life is precious and should be protected whenever possible (cf. Genesis 9:6, Exodus 20:13).

Additionally, the Bible calls on Christians to care for and protect the vulnerable, including the widows, orphans, and strangers in their midst (cf. James 1:27, Matthew 25:35-36). This includes providing a safe and secure environment for all members of the congregation.

The Bible instructs Christians to responsibly manage the resources and gifts bestowed upon them (cf. 1 Corinthians 4:2).

This includes taking measures to guarantee the safety and security of church property and the congregants.

The principles of protection, care, and stewardship found in the Bible suggest that creating a secure and welcoming environment for congregants is not only permissible but may also be seen as a responsible and faithful response to God's call. It is ultimately up to each church to determine the best approach to church security.

Churches need to evaluate their security needs and implement appropriate measures to reduce the risk of liability. This may include conducting risk assessments, developing security policies and procedures, providing adequate training for staff and volunteers, and maintaining appropriate insurance coverage. By taking a proactive approach to security, churches can help reduce liability risk and create a safe and secure environment for all.

The reality of our times
Once you have decided to create a security team, have a plan to be successful. The following can provide a roadmap for you as to how to move forward:

1. Assessment of any security needs - One plan does not fit all churches, so it might be beneficial to bring in local law enforcement or an expert in church security to determine security needs, identify possible threats, and provide a risk assessment (official report to operate under).
2. With that information, you can now create a security plan. This plan could discuss what is important, where cameras should be placed, how the church's leaders and security detail communicate with one another, and whether church staff should be trained to assist as needed.
3. This may be the most important aspect to cover — the church and security leaders need to understand each

other's roles and responsibilities. Suggested security responsibilities will be discussed later in this book. Each leader needs to know what is expected of them and the others. The adage of too many cooks spoiling *the broth* is in play here. During an incident, it is best practice for everyone to know what they should and should not be doing.
4. Communicating any type of security plans or expectations could make your congregation nervous. Slow and steady is the course. Later in this book, we will discuss plans to implement in case of crimes in progress or natural disasters.
5. Finally, one plan will not last forever, and unforeseen circumstances could dictate the adjustment, removal, or modification of existing policies and plans.

This type of top agreement between the leaders of the church and security should be considered a living document; it can and should be changed as your church grows. The expectation that everyone becomes a security expert is not realistic. Being prepared to protect your flock as best as possible is realistic and mandated biblically. 1 Corinthians 16:13 states, *"Be on guard; stand firm in the faith' be courageous; be strong."*

Should churches have security?
In a perfect world, the answer would be no. In a realistic world, the answer will always be yes. However, the truth is that not every church has security, and I would venture to say most home-based churches do not.

I have intentionally stayed away from splashing the pages of this book with headlines depicting the hate and attacks against churches. We all know those events happen. The information provided is not meant to cause undue fear but more of an eye-opener, a paradigm shift that is needed given the current attitude of socio-political polarization. Knowing how to respond to circumstances prepares one to react to unpredictable events or circumstances.

When talking about churches not in the home, the decision to have security is based on the individual church and its leaders. The recommendation is that any place of worship that is not home-based should have some level of security, regardless of its size and structural configuration. Unfortunately, churches, like any other public places or businesses, are exposed to and are vulnerable to potential risks resulting in injuries and crimes. By incorporating a security team, from one person to a multifaceted team, the church is taking active steps to deter potential threats that can result in injuries and crimes. Minimizing potential threats can increase the likelihood of ensuring the congregation's safety and being prepared in an emergency.

When the topic of security comes up in conversation, the decision to have any security should be made to protect the church and, more importantly, the congregants and everyone else in attendance.

How does the Bible define security?
The Bible does not provide an operational definition of the contemporary term "security." Nevertheless, numerous references related to this term can be found within the scriptural narrative, notably the mention of watchmen (cf. Isaiah 21:6).
Furthermore, the Bible offers guidance on attaining security and protection through the act of trusting in the Lord (cf. Proverbs 3:5-6), alongside the pursuit of wisdom (cf. Proverbs 2:10-11). These references imply the necessity of discretion and the importance of having a strategic plan in place (cf. Proverbs 21:31) to assist the church and its members during periods of uncertainty. The aforementioned considerations are pertinent to the establishment of a security team.

What is the role of the church in maintaining peace and security in society?

The church can play a significant role in maintaining peace and security. You are either pastoring a church, trained to pastor, or serving in a leadership role within your church. Whether you believe this is your calling or preparation for something else, according to God's plan, you are not meant to hold a position in idleness.

Churches are meant to be places where people come together to worship the Lord and help those who are seeking the Lord. Yet, the church does so much more. Churches help by maintaining peace and security in our society. They can meet the needs of the community (e.g., demographics, necessities, and partnering with other services and businesses).

Churches also provide so much more than spiritual well-being and support. The pastoral counseling prayers, understanding those in need, community engagement, uniting of the community, calling for peace in troubled times, and advocating for peace and justice for those who cannot advocate for themselves are what churches are called to do.

Without adequate security plans in your own house, how do you expect to grow and minister to others? Without taking care of the needs of the Congregation first, how could the church provide for and support those in the community, especially those who are suffering? As pastors, church leaders, and administrators, your calling demands that you take care of everyone, and this starts with those you are ministering to and praying for.

Does having a security team make a church feel less welcoming?

It stands to reason that if security policies and procedures are created and implemented properly, then a sense of trust, understanding, and safety will become part of the church and not just an outside identity. Consistency with security measures will quickly show your security team is well-trained, and everyone is welcome. Establishing clear communication is just as important. If you have an open line of communication with the members of your church, you will be able to explain the reasons for security, which will reduce anxiety and increase trust. An open display of firearms or security wearing uniforms is a great way to keep people from interacting with security. If possible, try to stay away from either.

The tone and approach of security will be seen and felt immediately. Both should show understanding and reassurance. Stand-offish security is a no-win prospect, and your congregants will start to become uneasy with them. If you hire an outside company, try to get them involved in activities or engage them in conversation.

Years ago, a church I was attending met at a local middle school in which a school employee had to be there to open the doors and lock up when we were done. We invited her to all the activities and food events and treated her like she was a member. And then one day, she decided to give her life to Jesus. That is why we positively engage people. This same concept will work for the security companies you hire.

The balance between security and being friendly is just that—a balance. One in which you may never achieve perfectly. There will always be obstacles that force security to look or act differently temporarily. That is okay. However, when whatever issue they were dealing with ends, they need to return to being the approachable and friendly members of the church.

Church security - protection with grace

As Christians, we are called to love one another and be gracious to all, even when it comes to church security. 1 Peter 4:8-9 states, *"Above all, love each other deeply, because love covers a multitude of sins. Offer hospitality to one another without grumbling."* (NIV) It is important to develop security protocols and communicate those to the church. Conventional wisdom states it is also important to implement and enforce those protocols in a professionally effective manner. These policies, implementations, and follow-through need to be accomplished with grace and compassion for all.

An effective way to implement protection gracefully is to:

1. Pray for both peace and protection for all who enter the church. Your prayers should seek wisdom in creating and implementing sound protocols and discernment while responding to potential threats or rising situations.
2. Talk with your church leaders and members. Listen to their concerns and voice your reasons.
3. Be prepared to provide information and resources showing the benefits of having a security team. Show them examples of successful programs at similarly situated churches.
   Note of caution - *Stay away from trying to scare your members or shocking them with horrendous news stories depicting carnage. This is ineffective and may drive people away from the church.*

   You may have noticed by now that this book does not contain shocking news stories or headlines. We already know what is happening in the world, and it does not need to be repeated; it just needs to be addressed.
4. Start small. This should be easy, given that most churches are small. Unless you are taking over a big established church, you will need to start small. This allows you to select and mentor the

best possible candidates who can later mentor and train new members. This is also where you can begin to learn how to develop emergency plans and coordinate with local first responders.
5. Build relationships with those working at the church, volunteering at the church, your congregants, and those who are visiting the church. Not everyone who walks through your doors is on the same financial, educational, or emotional level. There is not one perfect person in this world, which means we are all dealing with issues. Some issues may be solved in a day while others are much deeper and will never completely be eradicated. Regardless, knowing your congregation and showing them empathy will go a long way when handling any crisis that may arise later.
6. Communicate the need for security on the premises and the reasons behind setting up a security team. By letting your congregation know the whys, you are reducing their anxiety level and will make people feel more comfortable. Let them know the security is not a stand-alone unit, but they answer to the Pastor or Elders, depending on the organizational structure of the church. Let your congregants know security must follow certain protocols as well and there will be reviews of their incident reports and interactions with all. Being consistent with the protocols in place will show members that security is fair and professional.
7. To achieve protection with a mindset of grace, it is important to exercise discretion. Except in the case of a violent crime in progress, most situations can be handled in a manner that is respectful and compassionate. As mentioned earlier, maintaining a calm approach without yelling is

effective in most cases. Taking the time to listen to others is good common sense in human interaction. If there is an opportunity to offer assistance to help resolve the problem, then do so. Not every negative interaction warrants automatic removal from the premises. Showing compassion and empathy by helping when possible is crucial. This tone and attitude displayed will influence how individuals are perceived by the congregation.

If security needs to walk someone out of the building and off the property, the best approach is to be discreet and quiet. If a security member is arguing and escalating the situation or responding to every little insult with his or her own insult or bravado, that person should not be working security.

Approaching your members with sensitivity and respect will encourage and build relationships, which leads to a more secure and safe environment. Finding the right security team - one with the proper mindset, values, and training - will help create a safe and welcoming place of worship where people feel secure and welcome. Your security team needs to be welcoming, exhibit friendliness, and, most importantly, be approachable.

Balancing the security aspect of the job while showing hospitality is vital to success. Security personnel do not always need to look like they are angry at everything. A smile or handshake, when appropriate, can stave off many troubles. They need to remember first that they are there to get spiritually fed but also there to protect everyone.

Chapter Two
Organizing Church Security

Never assume everything is fine inside a church.

> *"Part of being a faith-based institution is having an understanding and faith that the Lord will or will not protect us from external/internal threats. When we attend Church, we are placing our security in the hands of the Lord... If the Lord sees fit to protect us, He will. If He sees fit to allow something to befall us, He will. We are fully in his hands."*
> Anonymous reply to Protection With Grace Survey

I agree with the above to some extent. God has a plan for every one of us, and we are not to step one foot over that boundary. And I agree that if something were to happen to us, it would still be part of God's plan. But that does not mean we should not protect our families, friends, and visitors, nor ignore basic warning signs that indicate danger. Much like we pull a child from stepping off a curb into traffic, the same applies to creating a safe environment for our congregants. To assume nothing terrible will happen to you, your congregation, or your property is not the correct servant-leadership attitude to possess. The attitude that nothing will happen is dangerous thinking. Recognize the need to provide a safe and comfortable environment for your members to attend and worship accordingly. It is your obligation.

God calls us to protect the flock. Most leaders have this in mind when they want to create a security element. They know they want one, but describing the duties and the roles can be convoluted or non-existent.

Acts 20:28-29
Be on guard for yourselves and for all the flock, among which the Holy Spirit has made you overseers, to shepherd the Church of God which He purchased with His own blood. I know that after my departure, savage wolves will come in among you, not sparing the flock

Churches and parishioners are not exempt from being the victim of violent and or property crimes. From 2014 to 2023, the FBI reported 28,088 related offenses as religious, occurring in or focused on churches/Synagogues/Temples,/Mosques. The following information was taken from the **FBI Hate Crime Data 2014-2023** link, addressing crimes based on religious bias:

Religious bias

Hate crimes motivated by religious bias accounted for 28,008 offenses reported by law enforcement. A breakdown of the biased motivation of religious-biased offenses showed:

Anti-Jewish	17375
Anti-Islamic (Muslim)	3331
Anti-Other Religion	1985
Anti-Catholic	1306
Anti-Multiple Religions, Group	961
Anti-Sikh	757
Anti-Protestant	736
Anti-Other Christian	495
Anti-Eastern Orthodox (Russian, Greek, Other)	437
Anti-Atheism/Agnosticism	166
Anti-Hindu	135
Anti-Buddhist	129
Anti-Church of Jesus Christ	124
Anti-Jehovah's Witness	71

The decision to have security?

Easy question – not so easy response. The first logical step is to designate a group of people who are willing AND capable of responding to security incidents and medical emergencies. This is what we call security. Whether they are paid personnel or volunteers, they will need training. If an outside company is hired, they will need to understand what is wanted and not wanted when it comes to dealing with various issues. The next step is to reach out to local first responders (Police and Fire Departments) to develop relationships and create an avenue for resources. Last, develop and maintain a set of security policies and procedures. This will need to be reviewed periodically to determine if changes are necessary. This could be based on new laws or old laws being removed, affiliation with church institutions, or could be based on moving to a bigger location. These policies and procedures must be read and signed off by anyone, regardless of volunteered or paid status, in security. No exceptions. The reason for security reading and signing the policies and procedures is that they now know the expectations set forth by the church.

Deciding to set up a security team at any level requires a review of your facilities and your programs. Do you meet in just a small building, or do you have multiple buildings? Do you operate in a neighborhood with young families, or are you situated in a retirement community? Who in the community are you providing for? These and other questions will help you and your team determine what type of security is needed. Below is a quick guide to help you understand what is needed for the size of your church. This guide is neither exhaustive nor all-inclusive, as each church is unique, and the needs of any given church are different.

The guide below cannot be accomplished in one day or one meeting. Decision-making requires prayerful consideration followed by discussions yielding fruitful deliberations with openness and willingness to make adjustments and modifications.

However, this guide provides a basic understanding of what is needed. This list is also to protect the church and its staff from predatory business practices seeking to sell over-priced services that may not be needed.

- [ ] Developing a security plan. This includes selecting security, protocols for addressing potential threats, response to emergencies, and, most importantly, communication protocols. Communication is everything.
- [ ] Conducting risk assessments is always a good idea. Your local police department can assist with this topic. *Protection With Grace LLC* can also be a source of assessment for the church. Risk assessments help identify what type of security measures are needed based on identifiable risks.
- [ ] Understanding the weak spots of your building(s) is non-negotiable. You, your leadership team, and your security team need to control access to any facility for the church. This can be easily accomplished by installing locks (according to local code), incorporating a key card or fob into critical areas (offices, nurseries), and other measures designed to restrict access to authorized individuals.
- [ ] Any staff or volunteers should be knowledgeable in the security protocols and emergency response procedures. They should receive training in how to identify suspicious circumstances or people and respond properly. Your local law enforcement agency or *Protection With Grace LLC* can assist with this training.

- ☐ Having a security video recording system is a must. Cameras can monitor facilities and parking lots and deter criminal activity. Camera positioning in strategic locations and visibility allows full coverage and can create a sense of security for the staff, congregants, and guests.
- ☐ Implementing a visitor check-in system allows monitoring of who and when people are coming in. Having a check-in system for the nursery is also essential.
- ☐ Once a plan is completed, meet with local law enforcement to discuss it so they are aware of the church protocols. This will help them if they need to respond to an emergency.

Creating and implementing a church security team can appear daunting at first. Yet, going through the process and thinking about what is needed right now instead of what is desired in the future will help create a safe environment for the church, its staff, congregants, and visitors.

The need to understand security

> *Our congregation doesn't see the need for an organized security ministry and doesn't want to be involved.*
>
> *Anonymous reply to Protection With Grace Survey*

You now have a basic understanding of the need for security as we discussed some basic concepts. The question then becomes – How do you approach the congregation and get them to see the need and importance of a safety ministry?

This can be a challenging process, and the number one argument coming back at you is *Why? Everything is working perfectly, and we have had no problems.*

This type of thinking can be linked to confirmation bias or the fact that they only seek out or want to hear information that conforms to their way of thinking. Besides being misleading at times, ignoring security issues can be downright dangerous.

The best security is when issues or disturbances are identified and handled without anyone knowing. This goes back to having security assigned who knows the law, has discretion, and is not looking to make a name for themselves.

Initiating a conversation with your members about the need for safety should occur in a non-threatening, non-confrontational manner. Ripping headlines from the news and shouting "SEE!" does nothing but scare people and make you look reckless. Instead, share your concerns with your members and listen to their experiences and perspectives. They may have come from another church with terrible security. Do not discount what they are saying or, more importantly, what they feel.

It is important to note, especially here, that when I mention a well-trained security team, I am not talking about people in military uniforms and tons of weapons marching around or kicking in doors.

I am talking about your members or an outside security company understanding your policies and procedures, and, while observant and friendly, will also respond appropriately to all situations.

Start small and get buy-in. Start with the nursery and work on ideas for checking in and checking out the babies. From there, move on to the kids and then the teens. Next thing you know, you will have people actively addressing various other issues. Once you get to the more complicated aspects of building a security team/policy, invite the local police in to help with some areas you may not be familiar with.

I can honestly say most churches are good about having the ability to lock doors leading to nurseries and classrooms. This will always be sound advice. But have you ever considered what else is in the rooms?

My wife has always used electrical outlet covers at the house, and with grandchildren running amok, it is easy to see why. Yet, I rarely see these covers at churches and have never seen them in the nurseries. I encourage you to make a small investment and purchase some type of outlet protectors.

Since we are on the topic of electricity and children, please take an honest look around your facilities for loose electrical cords or power bars that are full of plug-ins. Children are curious about the world around them, and if they can touch it, they will.

If you take your time, listen to your members, and start small, you will soon have a sustainable security team with buy-in from your members. Sustainability is crucial. You want a system in place that will withstand the turnover of security personnel, which in turn will ensure you have consistent and fair policies and procedures.

A church security survey?
Most churches I have worked with, been part of, or just have spoken with in the past have set up security teams or processes without input from the congregants. I understand that and have done it myself in the past. The argument is that people who know nothing about security know nothing about security. But what if we changed that paradigm just a bit and included the members in your security team's creation, goals, and mission?

One of the best ways to accomplish this is to create and distribute a church security survey. Filling out a church security survey can be of great importance when it comes to ensuring the safety and well-being of the congregation.

Here are several reasons why it is valuable to participate in such a survey, especially if it is intended for use in a book on church security:

1. **Identifying potential vulnerabilities**: A comprehensive security survey helps identify potential vulnerabilities within the church premises, such as weak access points, inadequate lighting, or areas that are prone to security breaches. By gathering information from the congregation, the survey can provide insights into areas that require improvement and allow for targeted security measures.

    Granted, because they were not trained in security measures, some of the responses may not apply or even be feasible. But a nugget of information may be brought forward that might have been missed.

2. **Tailoring security measures**: Different churches have unique security needs based on their size, location, and community. By participating in the survey, individuals can contribute valuable information that helps tailor security measures specific to their church's requirements. This customization ensures that security protocols and strategies are well-suited to the particular context, making them more effective.

3. **Encouraging a sense of ownership**: Involving the congregation in the security survey process fosters a sense of ownership and shared responsibility. When people have the opportunity to provide input and express their concerns, they become actively engaged in promoting a safe environment for worship. This can lead to increased vigilance, awareness, and cooperation among church members, enhancing overall security.

4. **Enhancing emergency preparedness**: The survey can include questions about emergency response procedures, picking up children during an event, and communication systems. By gathering this information, the church can assess its preparedness level and identify areas that require improvement. A thorough understanding of the congregation's knowledge and capabilities in emergencies can help create robust emergency response plans and ensure the safety of everyone present.

5. **Providing valuable data for analysis**: Collecting data from a security survey allows for the statistical or qualitative analysis and evaluation of trends, patterns, and potential risks. The information obtained can be used to identify recurring security issues, evaluate the effectiveness of implemented measures, and make informed decisions regarding resource allocation for security purposes. Additionally, the data can be anonymized and shared in a book to provide insights and best practices to other churches facing similar challenges.

Completing a church security survey is an opportunity to actively participate in creating a safer environment for worship. It empowers the congregation, helps identify vulnerabilities, and supports the development of effective security measures.

The surveys allow members to be part of something important; in return, they will be more receptive to and aware of security concerns.

> ****Learning concept –* **You never really know who in your church has certain skills or knowledge.**

So, what should this survey look like? It should look like any other announcement you put out to the members. The survey and its process should be in the announcements, discussed in small groups, and through everyday conversations. You decide to make the survey available through some type of web-based survey system or the old paper and tabulation method.

It's also important to tell the recipient of your survey approximately how long it takes to complete. Letting them know the amount of time can help respondents prepare for the level of commitment required. You can take the survey yourself or have several of your team members take it to compile a range of times that more accurately reflect this data.

Form Letter

Below is a suggested letter format that will ease the Congregation into the process.

Dear Church Members,

Ensuring the safety and well-being of our congregation is our top priority. To enhance church security, we are conducting a survey to gather feedback from all of you. Your participation is crucial for strengthening our security measures and creating a safe environment for worship.

This survey aims to assess our current security practices, identify vulnerabilities, and tailor our strategies to meet the needs of our community. Your insights and suggestions will help us address potential risks and improve our emergency preparedness.

All responses will remain confidential and anonymous, as the data will be aggregated to identify trends and areas for improvement. We encourage everyone, whether long-time members or newcomers, to participate.

The survey covers topics such as facility security, emergency response protocols, and your perceptions of safety within the church. Your contributions will help our church and provide insights for other faith communities facing similar challenges.

Thank you for your commitment to the safety of our church. We can create an environment where everyone can worship and fellowship with peace of mind. If you have any questions, please feel free to contact us.

Chapter Three
Roles and Responsibilities

What is the responsibility of church security?

The responsibility of security in a place of worship is to monitor, respond, act, and communicate irregular behavior or potential problems. This is done to ensure a safe and secure environment for members, visitors, or congregants. An effective team is a threefold function of (a) training, (b) mentoring, and (c) accountability concerning safety.

Monitoring the people in or around the church is the vast majority of the job while acting in the security role. A properly trained security member will know when something does not look right or can determine if problems are brewing (usually between people) and can respond accordingly. Monitoring also applies when a crime occurs. Depending on the situation, being a good witness might be better than putting oneself and others in further danger. This pertains neither to an occurring violent crime nor a crime in progress against a person but pertains to more property damage due to crimes occurring near the church.

The response will vary based on the circumstances. Sometimes, just being present is enough to deter problems or crime. Visitors may come to the church with a hidden agenda, only to realize the church has an active security team. Other times, engaging people in conversation is a form of response.

In my personal experience, when I worked at a convenience store while attending college, I was trained to say "hi" to everyone who walked through the door. This let the customer know I knew them and that it was good business practice. The same applies to churches. Let people know there is someone there who says hi and knows they are there. Another response is intervening in a situation before it escalates to a bigger problem. Again, we could spend countless hours and pages discussing the proper response to concerns and still only cover the tip of the iceberg.

I once supervised a newly promoted patrol Lieutenant who would call me for every minor issue. Finally, one night at 3 A.M., when he called again to reference an occurrence, I told him that if he needed my permission for every decision he made, I did not need him and that I could do the job myself. I then added that if he knew the Department's policy and directives, he could save us both a lot of time. He took this to heart, and the calls became less and less; he started operating at a level I knew he could and should handle.

Communicating is the key role and the Number One Rule of Success for any team or team member. Knowing how and when to communicate up or down the chain of command is essential. Having communication protocols in place will streamline this process and reduce the 'noise'. Sit down with your security team and draft out an understanding of when you should be notified, whether verbally, via email, texting, or by writing a report. This will save everyone time and allow you to hold them accountable as well.

Priorities for the safety and well-being of the congregants
Once you have set up your security team, be cognizant of the fact that church security should prioritize the safety and well-being of its congregants.

Providing relevant security information helps raise awareness and ensures that everyone can participate in maintaining a secure environment. Here is some security-related information that a church security team could consider sharing with congregants:

1. Emergency Procedures: Inform congregants about what to do in case of various emergencies, such as fires, medical emergencies, natural disasters, or security threats. Provide clear instructions on evacuation routes, assembly points, and any designated safe areas.
2. Suspicious Activity Reporting: Encourage congregants to report any suspicious behavior or activities they observe. Provide a clear method for reporting, such as a designated phone number or point of contact.
3. Personal Belongings: Advise congregants not to leave personal belongings unattended. Reminding people to keep an eye on their belongings can minimize theft and security breaches.
4. Parking Lot Safety: Provide tips for staying safe in the church parking lot, such as locking car doors, avoiding leaving valuables visible, and walking in groups when possible.

Child Safety: If the church has a nursery, children's program or Sunday school, provide guidelines for child drop-off and pick-up procedures. Emphasize the importance of checking identification for those picking up children.

Medical Assistance: Make sure congregants know the location of first aid kits and automated external defibrillators (AEDs). Provide basic information on how to respond to medical emergencies while waiting for professional help to arrive.

Evacuation Procedures: In case of emergencies like fires or building evacuations, ensure congregants know the quickest and safest ways to exit the building. Highlight any specific needs for people with mobility issues.

Online Security: If the church uses online platforms for communication or donations, advise congregants on best practices for protecting their personal and financial information online.

Digital Security: Encourage the use of strong, unique passwords for any church-related accounts and caution against sharing personal or sensitive information over email or social media. Some believe in the 30/60/90 rule, in which passwords should be changed every 30 days, 60 days, or 90 days. That might be too often, especially for smaller churches. The frequency of changing passwords is your decision, based on known cyber threats or employee turnover.

Awareness of Surroundings: Remind congregants to be aware of their surroundings inside and outside the church premises. Encourage them to report anything unusual or out of the ordinary.

Designated Contacts: Provide information about who to contact within the church in case of security concerns or questions. This could include the security team, ushers, greeters, or other designated personnel.

Security Personnel: If the church has security personnel or volunteers, make sure congregants are aware of their presence and their roles.

Training Opportunities: Offer security training sessions or workshops to educate congregants on how to respond effectively in different security situations.

Communication Channels: Establish clear communication channels for sharing urgent security-related information, such as through text messages, emails, or social media updates.

Community Involvement: Foster an environment where congregants look for one another's safety to encourage a sense of community responsibility.

Remember that while sharing security information is important, creating a welcoming and inclusive atmosphere is equally essential. Balancing security measures with the warm and open nature of a church community is key to fostering a safe and comfortable environment for all congregants.

Roles
A security team that knows and understands the assigned roles is an effective group of people who can act professionally and compassionately. Throwing a bunch of people into security and not discussing any expectations or providing any training is a waste of time; in essence, you have created nothing.

Knowing and understanding roles will increase professionalism and decrease the reaction time needed to stop a threat or provide life-saving first aid to an injured person. Granted, if you currently are a smaller church, there may not be a lot of roles to dole out. This means the responsibility of the security personnel will increase. Notice I did not mention that a smaller church will have fewer/smaller problems. Thinking like this is a flawed mentality and can lead to serious repercussions.

If you are the Senior Pastor of a small church, it is still important to sit down with your security team and discuss what is expected from them.

Most churches, especially smaller ones, will have volunteers working in numerous roles. I understand the need to wear many hats. The following graph indicates that in most churches, security members are also given other roles. These percentages are neither good nor bad; they are just a reflection of large and small churches.

Question: Does your security team perform other functions during service?

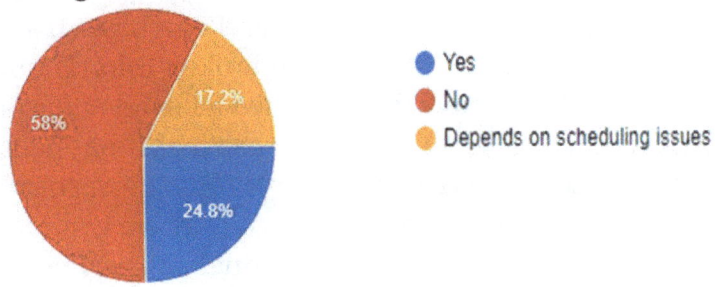

There needs to be a Security Leader with the organizational authority and experience to make security decisions. This person decides where others are positioned, responds, has the final say, and, if needed, interacts with either the Pastor or first responders. Having too many people acting like they are in charge looks terrible and can lead to further problems. The person who is the biggest is not always your best lead security person, so be careful of taking on this assumption.

If your place of worship is big enough (that is your decision), it is recommended that you assign people inside and outside the building. The inside people need to be positioned in places where they can view the most people or areas. The optimum positioning would be to have one inside the sanctuary and one near the main entry door. Depending on the layout of the building, think about positioning someone near the nursery or kids' room.

Some tend to think of outside security as being responsible only for vehicles inside the parking lot. Yes, that is part of it. Vehicles get broken into all the time, whether it is a crime of opportunity or a ring of thieves moving through an area. Crimes of opportunity arise when people leave items in the vehicle in plain view for the world to see.

It is mind-boggling to think back about all the reports I have taken from victims whose vehicles were broken into. Most stated they left something on the seat or failed to lock their doors. Leaving laptops, computer bags, cell phones, and purchases from stores in plain view begs for a vehicle to be broken into. Think about this - how many times have you attended a birthday party after church and decided to leave the gifts in the car? It happens more than most realize. As mentioned above, outside security entails more than just watching a parking lot. As they are walking around the premises, they should be conducting perimeter checks and looking for the following:

- Have doors been propped open or unlocked? If you have a stand-alone structure-type church, there may be many doors to check, but it needs to be done. If your church is in a retail area, you will have the front and back doors to check.
- Are the fire escape doors free from obstruction? People in a hurry tend to park where they can and will justify it to themselves. These vehicles need to be removed immediately, hopefully by the owners first.
- Is there a first responder activity in the area or coming onto the property? Traffic accidents, fire, and or police calls for service can oftentimes be very close to a church, and at times, those first responders might use part of your parking lot for responding units to set up command centers. Many times in my career, we set up command centers in parking lots, which can be overbearing to nearby businesses and places of worship. Being able to communicate what is happening to the security leader inside will help alleviate any worries or concerns about the unknown. Also, if a dynamic event happens outside (police pursuit, foot chase, chemical spill), people can be sheltered in place rather than let them exit the building(s).

- In most scenarios, outside security will usually be the first to meet with first responders. If the police or fire arrive because Security calls them, the outside security needs to be aware of problems inside so they can direct first responders to the appropriate location. They also help by keeping ingress or entry avenues clear for responding units to expedite their response.

2 Corinthians 8:21
For we are taking pains to do what is right, not only in the eyes of the Lord but also in the eyes of man.

Handling money (tithes, offerings, donations) should never be handled directly by anyone on the security team. It doesn't pass the smell test, and it looks bad when this occurs. The question then becomes - "Who is watching security?" Security should monitor the counting if your place of worship is large and verify with at least two others who count the money. If your place of worship is small, having a security representative count with another person who is not part of the security team is permissible. The spiritual leaders should be the ones overseeing the handling of all money.

Written policies must be established for collecting, counting, and depositing all monies, including unexpected donations. These policies also need to cover accounting, as most people can use the tithes and offerings as tax write-offs later. Once the money is collected, it must be deposited as soon as possible.

Keeping money 'hidden' until someone gets around to depositing it is lazy and does not comply with 1 Corinthians 14:40, which tells us that all must be done orderly. If money needs to be left at the building, investing in a good floor-mounted safe should help, as long as the safe is not in view for all to see.

The ideal security team member
Having laid the groundwork for the why (protecting first and then liability), the question becomes who should be selected to handle security. I cannot stress this enough: be careful when making these decisions. Just because someone is the biggest or has a military background or prior security experience does not mean they are the best choice.

Not every place of worship can afford a top-tier, well-trained security company or team to protect everyone and everything. In reality, as mentioned numerous times in this book, most churches will ask for volunteers. In my experience, new people will routinely ask to be assigned to security when asked where they would like to help out. There could be a thousand reasons for this, and one of those reasons could be evil. Be careful when selecting new people for positions of authority before vetting them.

While this list is not all-encompassing, it gives you a good understanding of where to begin. You may have police officers or active military in your Congregation that you think would be best based on their experience and training. This topic is discussed later in the book.

As mentioned before, most security teams at small churches are volunteers, and I would venture to say most have not had formal training. So, how does a small security team become effective?

Knowing that I could not handle every security situation by myself and with only a few volunteers to assist, I made an effort to talk with almost every able-bodied adult person at the church and asked them if they would be willing to stand behind me during a time of crisis (disruptions, drunks, etc.)

I explained to them I do not require anything from them or are they to interfere with my interactions. They were only to stand nearby to show solidarity and act as a force multiplier.

The thought process is that a person might think I am a soft target and can do what they want.

However, with a wall of people behind me, the thought process changes and they start weighing the odds. If you do not have a dedicated security team, ask your congregants if they would be willing to stand behind you and provide support when needed.

Hopefully, the following attributes will help guide you in asking the right people to assist with security:
1. Select someone who has buy-in. You need to select a person or persons who have buy-in to the place of worship. This means active members of the church are believers of the faith, are members of the place of worship, and participate regularly in faith-related activities, including tithing. These four attributes demonstrate a level of commitment and prevent the church-hopping people from landing a position of authority or an opportunist looking to exploit their new position.
2. Look for those with training and skills to handle emergencies, personal conflict resolution, and crisis management. These will be the least likely to aggravate or escalate a situation(s). Calmness and composure in a high-stress situation are so important. Security is not the place to panic when bad things happen. Remaining calm and composed helps ensure the right decisions are made during a crisis. It also has a calming effect on others, especially when giving them instructions.
3. The ability to adapt to ongoing, multi-faceted situations is highly desirable in a potential candidate. Some people can think of stressful happenings while others freeze. Look for those who can think and adapt, who can prioritize what is important now and what can be looked into later.
4. Those you are considering must consistently show some type of responsibility and reliability. It can be very frustrating to go through the process of selecting someone only to find out they are rarely at church.

5. Are they approachable? Please, do not select the most gruff or sourpuss person. This will not help your cause in having the best security available. An approachable demeanor and a smile do much more in setting the tone than someone who always looks like they want to punch someone.
6. Your selection should be respectful of the church, its members, staff, visitors, and vendors passing by. This respectful attitude will lead to a servant-type security volunteer who understands the need to create a safe and welcoming atmosphere.
7. Select someone who has decent communication skills. They need to communicate in a friendly and professional manner on any occasion. Effective communication skills allow them to have conversations with most people and will come into play during a crisis or when dealing with first responders. This will also help in dealing with first responders during chaotic times.
8. Consider someone who is discreet and does not feel the need to reveal all the secrets or try to bring glory to themselves. Not every church member needs to know everything.
9. Attention to detail is a must. It is imperative to distinguish between a threat and normal interaction. Security members will need to know the protocols and communication avenues. Attention to detail will help prevent potential security incidents.
10. Physical fitness is a desirable trait, but how will you measure that? Just because someone is big and seems fit does not make them a perfect candidate. Physical fitness is part of the selection, but do not start with this quality when looking for potential candidates. It is the aptitude to do things correctly that is more important.

Yet, there must be some level of physical fitness. It is not feasible to have someone working security who is dealing with a myriad of health issues. This does not mean they cannot be eyes and ears during critical times; it is just not prudent to put them in a position where tensions can escalate, or there is a chance of a physical encounter.

11. Diplomacy and good customer service skills should be added in. Whomever you select to run or be part of your security should be able to interact with staff, members, and visitors. This applies even if you hire an outside company. If they provide security officers who do not match what you are looking for, ask for replacements or find another company.

What are the duties of church security?

The duties of a security guard or team depend on location, the church size, and whether or not you hired an outside company to handle your security issues. Starting with the latter, you may reach a mutual conclusion about the duties if you hire a company. This will be determined by the contract negotiations and the agreements before actually hiring a company. If their values do not align with yours or their reputation might be considered heavy-handed, I recommend seeking a better fit that meets your needs. Spending time interviewing a company will help you decide if you even need them in the first place.

If you have a volunteer security team or even pay some of your congregants, they must understand the duties you listed in your policies and procedures manual. Below are some essential responsibilities to discuss with any new member or company coming in:

1. First and foremost, security members will comply with the church's policies and fulfill their obligations ethically, morally, legally, and faithfully following the church's tenets.
2. The primary duty is to protect the church and the congregation. Everyone entering, leaving, doing business, or in the parking lot must be monitored. Watching is the primary duty of any security member or team.

3. If you have cameras, a security member should monitor them. There is no sense in having cameras if they are for 'record only', which will only assist in the after-the-fact situation. Companies may try to sell you their camera system and say they can monitor it for you. That is your call, depending on your present location and budget. From my experience, there is a time delay from when a crime or incident happens and when the local first responders are called. The recommendation is to have security members monitor the cameras while in service or hosting events.
4. Responding to incidents will always be a duty of security. Whether it be an unforeseen medical emergency, a family disturbance, or an actual crime in progress, security must respond quickly and handle the situation professionally.
5. Security must establish relationships with local first responders. Safety is paramount because both need to know each other's responses and protocols. Establish those relationships as it will only help.
6. Security will ensure confidentiality regarding incidents, issues involving church members, and documentation.

The list provided earlier is not exhaustive, as each church has its own unique circumstances and requirements. Certain churches might require security personnel to accompany individuals to their vehicles or transport tithes to the bank for safekeeping. If specific points from the above list do not pertain to you, there is no cause for concern. Instead, focus on identifying the aspects that resonate with your experience and incorporate them into your participation in the church community.

Should security be identifiable?

The question that frequently arises in discussions, particularly in my own church community, revolves around the issue of whether security personnel should be identifiable. This decision is not straightforward and is influenced by several critical factors varying from church to church.

These factors include the specific needs of the church, the nature and frequency of regularly scheduled events, the overall size of the congregation, and the primary role that security personnel are expected to play within the church environment. It is essential to delve deeply into these elements to arrive at the most effective strategy for ensuring the safety and security of all attendees.

Advocates of uniforms for security personnel put forth several persuasive arguments in favor of their use:

Facilitated Identification: One key advantage of uniforms is that they allow for immediate recognition of security personnel.

This visibility not only reassures members of the congregation but also serves as a deterrent to potential threats by signaling that security is actively monitoring the environment. Having identifiable personnel can reduce instances of disruptive behavior and help prevent criminal activity from occurring within church premises.

Efficiency in Emergency Situations: In an emergency, the presence of uniformed security personnel becomes crucial for effective coordination. When first responders arrive, they can quickly identify who is part of the security team. This rapid identification is especially vital in larger churches, where distinguishing between staff and congregants can be challenging. Efficient response and management of the situation can be significantly improved when security personnel can be recognized at a glance.

Enhanced Sense of Security: Many congregants express that the presence of uniformed security staff significantly enhances their feeling of safety while attending services. For numerous individuals, especially those with safety concerns, seeing clearly identifiable security personnel provides much-needed peace of mind during worship. This sense of security can encourage attendance and participation in church activities.

If your church is considering the implementation of a uniform or identification system for its security personnel, it is crucial to establish a standardized approach. Allowing individual security personnel to select their own uniforms can lead to confusion and inconsistency, which is not a sound business practice. By adopting a uniform or consistent identification system across the board, the church can maintain clear guidelines on what is deemed appropriate attire for security staff.

This fosters a sense of professionalism and ensures that congregants and visitors can easily recognize who is responsible for their safety. A well-defined uniform will create a visible presence, enhancing the overall security atmosphere and promoting confidence among all attendees.

Of course, there are arguments against the use of uniforms by security personnel:

Maintaining a Welcoming Environment: Some churches prioritize creating a warm and inviting atmosphere that is accessible to everyone. In this context, security uniforms — particularly those that are military-style or overtly visible — can inadvertently foster a sense of tension or unease, especially among visitors who may interpret the presence of such uniforms as indicative of a lack of safety or security within the church. The added factor of visible firearms can heighten discomfort further, leading to a perception of hostility rather than protection.

Blending into the congregation: In certain circumstances, security personnel might be more effective if they blend in with the congregation rather than stand out. By dressing in casual, inconspicuous clothing, they can foster an atmosphere that feels approachable and non-threatening. This strategy can help security personnel engage more seamlessly with congregants and respond to situations more organically.

Financial Considerations: Implementing a uniform security system can impose additional financial burdens on churches, especially those with limited resources. The costs associated with purchasing uniforms, along with ongoing expenses related to maintenance, sizing adjustments, and ensuring that all security staff are properly outfitted, can strain budgets, particularly for smaller congregations. These financial constraints often necessitate tough decisions regarding the prioritization of resources.

Despite the differences on this issue, it remains vital for security personnel to be identifiable during critical situations. When emergencies arise, swift recognition by first responders of who constitutes security personnel can be the difference between chaos and effective crisis management. To reconcile the differing viewpoints on security visibility, several potential compromises could be considered:

Some churches choose to provide security personnel with discreet yet recognizable identification methods, such as badges, patches, or lanyards. These options allow security staff to be identifiable without requiring them to wear full uniforms, effectively striking a balance between maintaining a welcoming environment and ensuring safety and visibility during potentially critical situations. This approach fosters a sense of security while simultaneously preserving the overall atmosphere of the church. Other churches want security to wear normal clothes.

The decision on whether church security should wear uniforms depends on the church's goals, the safety needs of the congregation, and the atmosphere the church wishes to create. For many churches, having security personnel in uniforms can enhance visibility and authority, thereby improving overall security. However, for others, a more discreet approach may better align with their values.

It is essential to strike a balance between ensuring safety and maintaining the church's cultural and community-focused objectives. The decision regarding whether church security personnel should don uniforms is a significant one that should be carefully considered in light of the church's specific objectives, the safety needs of its congregation, and the overall atmosphere that the church aims to create and maintain.

At our church, I advocated for the implementation of security lanyards with photo IDs for the following reasons:

> 1. Visibility: It's crucial for people to easily recognize the security personnel and know who they are.
> 2. First-time Visitors: The presence of security lanyards ensures that newcomers to the church are aware that security is on-site and available to answer any questions they may have.
> 3. Critical Incidents: During emergencies, especially when first responders arrive, security needs to be easily identifiable. This facilitates a swift and efficient response and can help identify potential threats to minimize delays.

The photo IDs should include the following specifications:
- A recent headshot of the security employee on the front.
- The church logo on the front.
- The prominent display of "SECURITY" at the bottom of the front side in a font and color that ensures visibility.
- On the back, it is imperative to include the church address, phone number, and a signature from either the Senior Leader or the Security Supervisor. This provision aims to facilitate expedited communication in times of crisis by ensuring the prompt availability of essential contact information.

Ultimately, church leadership must evaluate their unique situation and community dynamics. Striking an effective balance between ensuring the safety of their congregation and preserving the church's cultural identity and community-focused objectives is crucial for fostering a secure and harmonious environment. If you are not sure which direction to take, go to prayer first. Also, ask your congregants and your employees what they prefer. Their answers might surprise you.

Chapter Four
Communication

The power of a team speaking with one voice!

I have always been a proponent of a team speaking as one. The message must be communicated, received, understood, and implemented. As leaders, having the team, staff, members, and volunteers speak in one voice is important. Communication inconsistency within a church team can cause confusion, division, and inefficiency. This can lead to disconnected efforts, overshadowing the shared mission and creating an unpleasant experience. Without a unified voice, the team may struggle to convey a clear message, diminishing their impact and effectiveness and weakening trust and community.

The same applies to security personnel (additions or new areas of concern). If your team is speaking about different missions or future directions, you need to reel them in and re-explain the path forward. Having a cohesive team with a shared vision and clear communication protocols is essential for effective church security. This means that all team members should be on the same page when it comes to their roles and responsibilities and their expectations for how to handle potential security situations. By speaking with one voice, the church security team can also establish trust and credibility with the congregation and other stakeholders, such as local law enforcement agencies and fire departments.

Church security teams should regularly review and update their policies and procedures to ensure everyone is aligned and working towards the same goals.

Effective communication, collaboration, and a shared commitment to safety can help create a unifying and agreed-upon culture of security that protects the church and its members.

Identify a spokesperson for the church during emergencies

The lead Pastor or an Elder is usually the designated individual who is responsible for representing the church to the public and media for normal activities or media requests. But, have you considered who that person would be during a time of crisis (victim of crime, tragedy, or accident)? If you decide you will be that person, great. Explain your decision to the security team, then move on to the next section. Alternatively, you could consider one of the following two options:
a) Assign your security supervisor to handle the details of the crisis, while you serve as the primary point of contact for general inquiries, comments, and concerns related to the church's activities, events, and other matters; or
b) Assign your security supervisor to only discuss the crisis in broad terms, stating that the church will make an official statement at a later time. Either way is fine – just have a plan before ever needing one.

If you decide to use the spokesperson route, he or she should be someone who is well-versed in the church's mission, values, and policies and who can effectively communicate the church's message to various stakeholders. They should have strong communication and interpersonal skills and be able to handle sensitive or controversial issues with confidentiality, tact, and diplomacy.

In addition to representing the church to the public and media, the spokesperson may also serve as a liaison between the church and other organizations, such as law enforcement or local government agencies, in security or emergency preparedness matters.

The church needs to have clear guidelines and protocols for how the spokesperson should communicate with the public and media and how they should handle sensitive or confidential information.

By having an official spokesperson, the church can ensure that its message is communicated effectively and consistently and that the public has accurate and reliable information about the church's activities and events.

Security Communication

The size of your church will determine what type of communication system you have. Smaller churches can use face-to-face communication, while larger churches may have to use phones or radios. No matter what type of system you incorporate, the basics concerning communication are the same. The importance of clear and concise communication is essential when encountering potential problems or medical episodes. Clear speech reduces the risk of miscommunication and decreases the response time for law enforcement and or medical responders. In emergencies, even small misunderstandings can have serious consequences. Speaking calmly helps ensure that the intended message is accurately received and understood by all parties involved.

If you decide to issue radios to Security, Nursery, or parking lot volunteers, all must understand that the radios are not used for everyday conversations. Only communication that is essential to keeping the congregation safe should be utilized. The typical radio used by churches can usually be heard by non-church members nearby. This means that sensitive or confidential information should not be relayed over the radio. If such information needs to be transmitted, less is better. Limiting conversations over the radio ensures that when the radio is used, most will immediately understand that some emergency needs to be addressed.

Write emergency scripts for the Pastoral Team

Fortunately, emergency scripts do not garner much discussion and are rarely needed. However, there are times, in all sizes of worship places, when the pastor or pastoral team needs to be notified immediately.

I have spoken with my Pastor about this very topic. We worship in a very small setting, so getting his attention is not the issue, and communication can happen quickly. I have asked my security volunteers to contact the Pastor if I am handling emergency issues that could affect the congregation (fights, major vehicle accidents on property, police activity near the entrance, etc.).

Regardless of how big or small your place of worship is or where it is located, you need to have a plan to notify your Pastor if there is an emergency while preaching. Having a mechanism to calmly and discreetly notify the Pastor is crucial in avoiding disruptions or panic during service.

If you have time and the emergency is not critical to the safety of others in attendance, use ushers, staff, or greeters who are located near the Pastor. They will be in a good position to relay a note to the Pastor. Passing a message to the Pastor, if feasible, during the key moments in which there is a slight break from worship to sermon to prayer is desired. Security should assess the situation first if a critical incident or emergency occurs. Is the emergency critical, and does it need immediate attention from security? If there are chances of a threat to lives, immediate action must be taken first. When possible, call 9-1-1 or have someone else call. Property crime is not considered an emergency, nor is it classified as a violent crime. If security observes these types of crimes outside the building(s), they should call 9-1-1 and not bother the Pastor. If the property crime is happening inside (theft or vandalism), security will assess the need to notify the Pastor during service.

Most fair-sized churches use technology to assist with keeping the worship team and the Pastors on track. Both use screens located in the back of the worship area.

If there is a problem or an evacuation needs to happen, a message on the back screens **only** will give the Pastor ample time to read, comprehend, and then advise the Congregation.

If the technology is not there, then non-verbal clues are the best. My Pastor and I discussed the clue from me to him, which would trigger an interruption in service. You and your security team will need to do the same. Whatever the signal is, try to be in the line of sight with the Pastor so the message is received immediately. If this might be a hurdle, then a small flashlight or even the flashlight from a cell phone may help.

Finally, if the situation is so drastic (active shooter, natural disaster, fire, and so on), discretion goes out the window, and the need for the Pastor to know is paramount. If you have set up a security plan and discussed it with the leadership team, everyone should be working on moving or assisting everyone in the building in the same way to pre-determined locations.

Remember, rarely will an immediate message be given to the Pastor. However, if needed and if security has time, it should be done discreetly, and disruption to the service should be kept to a minimum. By showing calm in the lesser emergencies, confidence and trust will grow in your security team.

During a true emergency, the leadership and security must remain calm. Showing signs of panic will only instill panic in others, which, in turn, will lead to more problems. Having an actual script available and nearby will help tremendously during critical incidents.

During medical emergencies, a possible script could be as follows:

> *"Attention staff, congregants, and visitors, we have a serious medical emergency. If you have medical training, please stand up so ushers (or security) can direct you to the location. Everyone else, please remain seated."*

In case of a fire, the following is to the point:

> *"Attention staff, congregants, and visitors, we have a fire emergency located near (list room, building, etc.).*
>
> *Please follow the directions of the security team and evacuate the building immediately and calmly. Follow all exit signs and proceed to the rally points outside the building."*

OR

> *"We have activated the fire alarm, and the fire department has been notified and is en route. Please exit the building using the nearest exit."*

In either scenario, if you have classrooms for the kids or nurseries for the babies, you will need to modify the statement, depending on the location of the fire, to let parents know they need to get their children or that someone will be escorting them out to the rally point.

If your place of worship is located in parts of the country that receive severe weather, a possible script could include:

> *"Attention all, a severe weather warning has gone into effect. Please use the designated areas of the building(s) to shelter in place. Stay away from doors and windows as well. Water will be brought to you."*

As with fire emergencies, parents will want to be with their children. Unless there is a tornado on the ground outside your front door, let the parents pick them up and comfort them in the designated safe places.

It is important to have clear and concise communication during emergencies. The actions during a critical event will not always flow the way the procedure is written or how the training is conducted. However, it is better to have a general understanding of the concept of critical communication than to have nothing in place. Constantly reviewing the plans, along with practice, will help eliminate some of the confusion during critical times and will show the Congregation you care about their safety.

Different church security teams communicating with each other

In the chart below, it is interesting to see that most church security teams do not communicate or even know other security teams from nearby locations. I figured this was the case, but wanted confirmation from the Protection With Grace, LLC, survey, which was created to determine if I was right or not. But the question is, why? Why don't churches and their security teams get to know and build relationships with other teams? I do not believe churches are meant to operate in isolation in the world or remain in a bubble, without developing relationships with other places of worship. I also do not believe churches should be cliquish and only work within their own small area.

Question – Is your Church security team in contact with other local Church security teams?

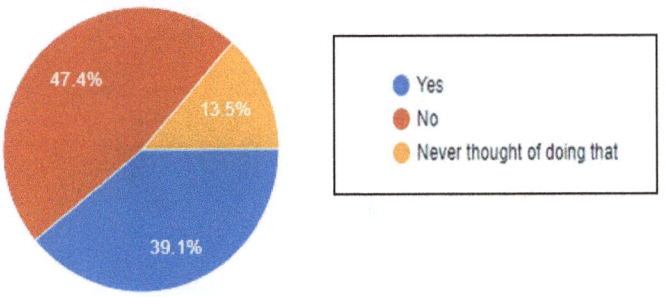

The same thought process can be applied to security teams. Church security should reach out to nearby churches, synagogues, mosques, branches, temples, gurdwaras (Sikh temples), etc. This list is not inclusive, as there are many religions. Regardless of ideology, communication is essential between all security teams.

Communication can reduce or prevent misunderstandings, respond better to emergencies, have resources nearby for those who need particular assistance, and, more realistically, share information about those bouncing from worship center to worship center, intent on either causing harm or conducting scams.

The question is then – How do we accomplish this? The answer is quite simple. Be the first to facilitate meetings. Reach out and let them know you would like to host a small working lunch with the hopes of establishing communication channels and protocols of when and how to communicate. Simply passing around a sign-in sheet for attendees to list their names, emails, and phone numbers (if they feel comfortable doing so) is a great first step. This form can be copied at the meeting and passed out to all.

This idea of reaching out to other security teams does not equate to answering to or following other teams. It is not meant to give up your autonomy. What it does accomplish is create relationships with other places to better the community and your church. Period.

Chapter Five
First Responders and the Law

It is not your security team's job to be the police.
Most church security volunteers or paid companies are not law enforcement officers, and it is not their job to act or react like the police. Some states have laws about what constitutes a security officer. A church security team member's job is to be visible and respond to those who need assistance. If needed, they can and should deter those who wish harm on others and respond to emergencies when needed.

I strongly recommend that your security work closely with local law enforcement and attend any training those departments offer. By building relationships with local law enforcement, you are opening the door to discuss safety and response protocols with them. By building relationships with them, you are now in a position to offer them the use of your facilities to train. Asking the local police and fire to use your facility to train (under your guidance and limitations) can help in identifying potential security gaps and provide opportunities for safety tips to further keep the congregation safe. All of this will greatly assist both you and first responders if the need to respond arises, as they will be familiar with the building and rooms, and it creates relationships with the church staff.

This is a perfect time to discuss what security can and cannot do. Regardless of any crime or infraction being committed, **ALL** people on U.S. soil are covered by the U.S. Constitution.

This means the police and security personnel cannot just do what they want to other people (illegal searches, illegal detainment, putting their hands on them, searching vehicles). Church security needs to understand what they can and cannot do when operating in that particular role.

In Nevada, to be considered a sanctioned security guard, one must take classes for the following topics:

1. Rights of citizens

2. Powers of arrest

3. Limits of authority

4. Recognizing noncompliance with laws

5. Recognizing noncompliance with regulations

If you have church members who volunteer to work security at your church, it is recommended that you research your state and local laws to learn the dos and don'ts of their function. (There is a link to all the States' laws or statutes in this chapter.) Reaching out to your local police department may help you obtain a clear understanding of the laws in your area.

I understand most churches will not send their security team to classes, as it is not feasible. However, whoever you select must understand their limitations, as they cannot make arrests or illegally detain people. The general rule of thumb is that if a crime is being committed, intervene if necessary to prevent physical harm and then call the police. If security observes a property crime occurring, be a good witness and call the police. Period.

If the conversation of carrying restraints (handcuffs, zip ties, hobbles, etc.) comes up, the recommendation is not to allow any restraints by church security. The only exception to this would be if you had current law enforcement officers who are trained in the use of restraints.

The improper application of restraints can lead to serious injuries, resulting in civil lawsuits. If your church can hire a company to handle your security needs, they will be responsible for the training and correct application of any restraints.

Being a good witness means you have been observant and know what is going on around you, and are aware of any potential threats. Focusing on details, such as the make and model of a car, the license plate, color, and type of clothing, is someone acting suspiciously, any nuances (speech, a unique gait, odors), and others will significantly help in either preventing a problem or properly communicating to the police when they arrive. Being able to document what an eyewitness has seen is just as important as physically intervening, at times. The proper documentation of incidents will be discussed later in this book.

Should churches work with first responders?

That answer should be a resounding YES! Local places of worship and local police working together help lessen the chances of miscommunication, identify and address community issues, and create positive relationships. From my experience, I have seen the benefits of places of worship interacting with the police with excellent results.

Unfortunately, most responses from the survey showed that regular interaction with first responders was not the norm. The chart below shows a disparity in worship centers' interactions with local first responders. 32% of the respondents stated they occasionally invite local responders, 11.7% stated they are rarely invited, and just under 3% stated they only interact with local first responders when invited. I encourage you to help bring up those percentages to where most places of worship invite and interact with them.

Question – Does your Church invite or interact with local first responders in your community?

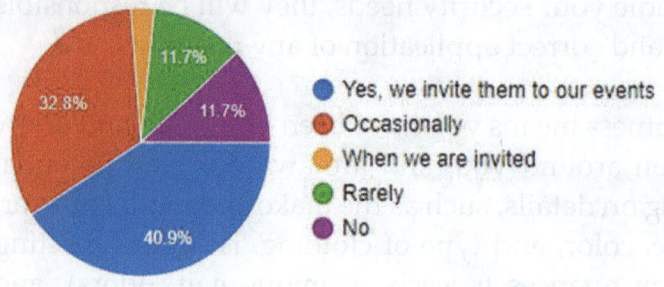

Churches should work with their local first responders to protect their congregation and visitors even more than they thought possible. As you can see from the above chart, some churches regularly invite first responders to their events, others invite them sometimes, some rarely invite them, and some have no relationship with them.

The reasons for inviting them are multi-faceted.

1. First responders are always seeking positive events to attend and connect with the community. Take advantage of that and invite them. Most departments will show up with officers or firemen in uniform, with their respective vehicles. Kids love to see the cars and trucks and love to sit in them and play with all the electronics.

2. Having first responders attend your events gives them a view of the inside of your facility. Knowing the layout gives them the advantage in case they do need to respond to a critical incident.

3. Having the relationships in place will help in scheduling training for your staff, volunteers, and security personnel. They will meet with you and

discuss different levels of emergency plans, preparedness, and procedures.

Knowing what they will be looking for when they arrive and training your security team to act and respond when first responders are on property will eliminate potential pitfalls and speed up the process to a conclusion as to why they are there in the first place.

4. Working with first responders allows you to create more relationships that can effectively and directly help the community. In the church I attend, the associate Pastor began communicating with the local law enforcement agency with the hopes of working on mutual community issues. Fast forward to today, and the Police Department is dropping off massive amounts of food, which in turn, is used to further and grow the feeding of the residentially challenged. So much food has been coming in every week that we were forced to seek a sponsor to buy a deep freeze (Remember, we are a small church).

While working as a Captain for the Las Vegas Metropolitan Police Department (LVMPD), I worked and visited many places of worship and created and designed many community events with all denominations. I have seen the benefits firsthand; from a witness coming forward with information about a homicide during a community event, or a Pastor showing up at a gang member's house to talk him out of committing a retaliation shooting. I worked with a local church to help a nearby apartment complex that was experiencing numerous crime-related issues. Through the Police Department's efforts and those of the church, a Bible study was established in that apartment complex, and people began attending that particular church.

Along with many other police agencies, the Las Vegas Metropolitan Police Department (www.lvmpd.com) uses a national program called Rebuilding Every City Around Peace (RECAP) to interact with and build relationships with the community. Both share information and resources to reduce crime and negative social issues in the community while strengthening neighborhoods.

Places of worship have assisted law enforcement across the nation in a variety of ways for years. Unfortunately, that does not make for good headlines, so little is printed or discussed. In Las Vegas, the relationships between the police and the different denominations are very strong. Both have worked very closely to monitor and assist with the protests the nation has experienced. They helped the police immensely by showing up and sponsoring events for families of fallen officers. They have reached out to the department's precincts or bureaus to lend a comforting ear to officers and civilian employees after tragedies. Religious establishments can create a positive environment for officers and their families and help them heal. And, as you may have guessed, some officers and their families started attending those places of worship.

The Fire Department is a great resource to invite out to special events as they will bring the big fire engines and let the kids climb on them, hand out stickers, and generally provide added entertainment value to your events. Most fire departments offer some type of training in first aid, CPR, and safety awareness classes. This includes barbecue safety, carbon monoxide safety, holiday cooking, firework safety, etc. If your local fire department offers any type of emergency preparedness or emergency management programs to join, I encourage you to take a serious look at those as well. The worst-case scenario is that you will have a better understanding of the capabilities of the fire department.

The real benefit of inviting first responders to your events is relationships built and fostered for years to come. Having both on-site establishes face-to-face relationships with you, your congregation, and your security team. Another benefit is the first responders will get to know the layout of your building(s) which helps during critical incidents. I know both police and fire are always looking for new places to train (building searches, K9 searches, etc.) Offer to let them train in your house of worship, with security on hand to remind them of any off-limit locations inside.

If your place provides food after services, invite the local responders to come out and join you during this time. Trust me, first responders are always looking for safe places to eat, and what a great way to interact with those sworn to protect us. By inviting them, they may find your church welcoming and start attending with their families.

If your church does not regularly invite first responders to your events, please reconsider this stance. I encourage you to engage with them to create positive outcomes for the community and to further protect your congregation.

If your church is not big enough to operate or create events, then go to them. Almost every agency these days has events churches can participate in, be it training, helping the community heal after a tragic event, participating in responses to certain calls, or by being involved in citizen boards. I believe you will quickly see that the rewards are much greater than trying to do everything by yourself.

Ask the police to conduct walkthroughs of your church

Reaching out to local law enforcement and inviting them to your place is always a good idea. Invite them over, as an individual or a squad, feed them, and give them a tour of the facilities.

Ask them while doing this if there is anything they see that might pose a danger or a threat to the congregants or staff. They can identify possible vulnerabilities and give feedback on ways to remove the vulnerability or reduce it. They can sit down with you and work on emergency plans as well. Offer them the space to train, with restrictions. They usually will welcome this opportunity

When to call 9-1-1 or 3-1-1
The two numbers serve two distinct responses. Your security team must understand the difference. The general rule of thumb is that 9-1-1 is for a critical emergency, and 3-1-1 is to report a non-violent crime.

A person should call 9-1-1 immediately in any situation that requires urgent medical, police, or fire response. Here are some examples of emergencies that require calling 9-1-1:
1. Medical emergencies: This includes symptoms of a heart attack, stroke, severe injury, difficulty breathing, severe allergic reactions, seizures, and any other medical condition that requires immediate attention.
2. Fire emergencies include any situation where a fire endangers people or property, such as a house fire or a wildfire.
3. Police emergencies: This includes situations such as a crime in progress, domestic violence, a suspicious person or vehicle, or any other situation where a police officer is needed urgently.
4. Natural disasters: These include situations such as floods, tornadoes, hurricanes, or earthquakes, where people may need immediate assistance or rescue.

In general, if someone is experiencing a life-threatening emergency or witnessing a dangerous situation, they should call 9-1-1 immediately.

It is important to provide as much information as possible to the emergency dispatcher, including your location and any relevant details about the emergency, to help ensure that the appropriate response is dispatched quickly.

In most cities in the United States, 3-1-1 is the non-emergency phone number that citizens can call to request information, report non-emergency situations, and access municipal services. You should call 3-1-1 when you need assistance or information related to city services that are not emergencies.

Here are some examples of situations when you might want to call 3-1-1:
1. Report a non-emergency crime, such as a stolen bike or vandalism.
2. Report a noise complaint or other nuisance.
3. Report a stray animal or request animal control services.
4. Report a non-emergency health or safety hazard.

Remember that 9-1-1 is the number to call for emergencies such as fires, crimes in progress, or medical emergencies. If you are unsure whether to call 9-1-1 or 3-1-1, it's always better to err on the side of caution and call 9-1-1.

What should security do when the first responders arrive?

If first responders are called, security can take specific actions to decrease response time to those in need or injured and prevent miscommunication. It starts with clearly communicating when calling 9-1-1 while providing the details and location of any incident. Telling dispatch who you are and what you are wearing will go a long way in eliminating potential misidentifications or mishaps.

Question—Do members of your security team even know the church's physical address? If your church is big enough, most first responders might see the address.

But if you are a start-up church or operate out of a commercial complex, you will need to give them an accurate address. If applicable, knowing the address and the suite number can greatly decrease response time.

When the police or fire department does show up, when it is safe to do so, immediately identify yourself and your role. Having a visible, break-away lanyard, indicating you are part of security, will help in this area. The worst thing a security member can do, especially if not in uniform and not trained, is to run towards the police with a gun in their hand. I know what you are thinking – "Does that happen?" or "Are people that dumb?" The answer to both is YES! Security needs to understand that things happen very quickly during critical incidents, and mistakes can be made.

The best way to eliminate a potential mistake is by holstering a firearm, any type of electronic control device, etc., before meeting with the police. Once you identify yourself, you should immediately follow any command they give you. By doing so, you reduce the risk of an accident, and you are showing them you are cooperative. All of these recommendations help speed up their response time to address the real problem.

Once you have established contact with the first responders, you can then provide information and show them the location(s) of where the problem is happening, where the injured people are located, and the people who have committed crimes. Comply with law enforcement instructions promptly and without resistance. If there are concerns or questions, those can be addressed later, but it's essential to prioritize immediate cooperation. The quicker first responders realize you are security, the quicker they can address the reason why they are there.

I listed earlier the best qualifications for a security member to have, and one of those was the ability to communicate.

In situations in which a crime is ongoing, has been committed or there is an injury or a medical episode, clear, concise, and accurate information from security to first responders is critical. By remaining calm and professional, security can demonstrate they understand what is happening and can help in keeping others calm. Screaming into the phone with 9-1-1 will only slow the response down. Giving information slowly and calmly is faster than being asked to repeat what was said.

Talk to your LEO Congregation
In all the churches I have attended, the same question is asked once they find out I work in law enforcement: *"Do you want to help with security?"* That is a fair question and one that is asked frequently. However, the answer may not be simple.

For starters, law enforcement employees work 40+ hours every week dealing with other people's problems, crime, and bad people. In my experience, the things they see and encounter drive them to seek peace and a bit of reprieve from the dregs of society. Being in church allows them to catch their breath and get some much-needed mental rest. A lady who used to attend the same church as I attended was an elementary school music teacher. The call went out for volunteers to help with the Worship Team, and I noticed she did not sign up. When I asked her why not, she replied that she deals with the music for over 40 hours every week and did not want to add additional meetings, practices, and sets to her agenda. She wanted to come to church to get fed spiritually. The same applies to law enforcement. Please understand, some law enforcement employees just do not want to help with security.

Another reason some law enforcement employees do not work in security is directly related to a department's policy.

The Las Vegas Metropolitan Police Department does not allow its officers to work in private security. Below is a section of their policy that states the following:

LVMPD Outside Employment (5/101.35)

Occupations for which outside employment will not be granted include, but are not limited to:

1. Sales, service, and distribution of retail liquor, medical, or recreational marijuana as the primary function of outside employment. For example, a bartender whose primary responsibility is distribution of liquor will not be allowed. However, a food server who occasionally serves liquor as part of his duties would be acceptable. No employment of any type, consultation, or subcontracted work is permitted at medical or recreational marijuana businesses.

2. Responsibilities are directly related to gaming functions (i.e., dealer or other games of chance utilized in the gaming industry; collection of monies from gaming activities; slot machine mechanic; supervision of the same).

3. Private detective, security guard, repossession, or collection.

4. Cab driver, limousine driver, rideshare driver (Uber, Lyft, Sidecar, etc.).

5. Locksmith

6. Accident reconstruction

7. Any position which may require the carrying of a weapon (except department approved Special Events)

8. Consultation or expert witness testimony for any police business which may conflict with the best interest of the LVMPD (evaluated on a case-by-case basis).

(2022). Las Vegas Metropolitan Police Department Policy. ,(157-158), . http://www.lvpmsa.org/Forms/Dept.%20Man%207-14-07.pdf

The Phoenix Police Department has the same policy:

> 1019.3.1 OUTSIDE SECURITY AND PEACE OFFICER EMPLOYMENT
>
> No member of this department may engage in any outside or secondary employment as a private security guard, private investigator or other similar private security position

(2021, Summer). Phoenix Police Department Policy. https://www.phoenixoregon.gov/sites/default/files/fileattachments/police/page/141/phoenix_pd_policy_manual.pdf

When I was working full-time, in law enforcement, I was never interested in working in church security simply because I was not able to do so. Even while having the policy in place, another question asked at times was, *"Well, could you at least just kinda check the parking lot or other areas for us?"* or words to that effect. Please, in my view, putting undue pressure upon law enforcement professionals within the congregations is likely to create tension and discord, which is ideally something that a church should not embrace. If they tell you they cannot perform any type of security work, there is a good reason for that response, and the best way to deal with such a response is to be gracious, express gratitude for their consideration, and move on to find others to help.

Some departments do allow their officers to work security, but the request needs to come through official department channels, and there is a certain wage that needs to be paid to off-duty officers. New York City Police Department states, *"All Paid Detail police officers are considered off-duty, acting as private contractors."*. Their policy continues by noting:

> *All police officers carry with them full law enforcement powers and are expected to perform police-related duties only. They do not carry or issue summonses. They are subject at all times to NYPD rules, regulations and standards of conduct.*

(2016, Summer). PAID DETAILS. https://www.nyc.gov/html/nypd/downloads/pdf/public_information/nypd-258_paid_details_2016-06-16.pdf

To use officers from the NYPD, the request must be made through the department's offices. However, places of worship or other businesses cannot specifically ask for certain officers.

And still, others have different ways of addressing this issue. The Seattle Police Department does not allow its officers to own their security businesses and prohibits employment that, "...*requires access to police files, records, or services as a condition for employment."*.

(2019, Spring). 5.120 - Off-Duty Employment. *Seattle Police Department Policy,* (),. https://www.seattle.gov/police-manual/title-5---employee-conduct/5120---off-duty-employment

> Proverbs 11:3 The *integrity of the upright guides them, but the unfaithful are destroyed by their duplicity.*

It is important to understand officers cannot randomly run people or license plates, while on or off duty. Why do I bring this subject up? Once again, it is based on past experiences. This happens more than people realize, and it is usually based on church officials wanting to help a member of the congregation who is facing relationship/marital problems. The request can also come from other members of the church. Either way, people often do not know or understand the rules of accessing this type of information. Officers can be suspended or terminated if attempting to access criminal history when it is not based on their job as a police officer. Please do not put them in a position that would be unethical. Most officers will tell you when they can and cannot do something. Accept their answer and move on. Hence, it is very important to be willing and able to exercise healthy boundaries.

Other things to consider when asking if their members/officers will work security:

1. Will you be paying them? If so, there may be some additional red tape and procedures you must abide by. The department usually sets these. For example, the New Orleans Police Department has a set wage schedule and requirements for requesting officers. Click on or search the link for further information, *Office of Police Secondary Employment* **https://nola.gov/next/police-secondary-employment/home/**
2. If you are not paying them, is there any remuneration or benefits given to the volunteer security team that may interfere with the officer's departmental policy?
3. By pointing them out as law enforcement employees and asking them to be part of security, you might be creating a very dangerous situation for that person and their family members. The fact is that not everyone who goes to church is there for the message or brings the best intentions. We do not know what experiences people have had in the past that can make them want to lash out at police officers and/or their families. Some are there for other nefarious reasons. Be aware that groups are out there collecting personal information on law enforcement employees (commissioned and civilian). Outlaw motorcycle gangs and other organized criminal elements are notorious for trying to gather information. If you want to ask if law enforcement employees would be interested in helping with security, please do so in a private manner. This way you can demonstrate discretion while honoring their privacy.

4. Understand that there are mainly two types of law enforcement employees: Police and Civilian workers. They do not have the same training or experience. The police are better trained to handle critical incidents, while the civilian workers mainly deal with administrative duties within the police department. Just because someone says they work for a police department does not make them the ideal candidate. The church and its security team still need to ask the right questions when bringing others to the team.

Even if the law enforcement employees do not wish or cannot be part of the church's security team, more than likely, they will self-initiate at the first sign of trouble or onset of a critical incident, and in most cases, probably will tell you there is a problem before it begins. A local Las Vegas Pastor told the story of a knife-wielding man who entered during services and started waving a knife around. Before anything terrible happened, several off-duty officers jumped up and handled the situation quickly and quietly without harm to anyone, including the man with the knife. When officers do take appropriate action, they are usually covered by their policies and laws. And in the above case, this would have been true if they had to use any force.

State laws and links
It has been my experience that most people really do not understand laws and their elements. Without turning this into an introduction to the criminal justice system, it is important to note that each crime must have specific elements. As my wife teaches, elements of a crime are similar to a recipe – you must have certain ingredients to make a cake. The same applies to crimes. State criminal laws delineate the specific legal elements that define offenses such as burglary and trespassing. These laws can differ significantly between jurisdictions, presenting unique challenges and considerations for each community.

For churches, understanding these regulations is vital not only for recognizing when a crime has taken place but also for determining the appropriate response and ensuring compliance with legal obligations.

Moreover, being well-versed in legal definitions and statutes equips church leaders to respond effectively to any incidents that may arise. This preparedness can significantly diminish the risk of escalation and may help avoid misunderstandings with law enforcement.

Finally, understanding the intricacies of these laws can help churches navigate potential legal pitfalls, ensuring that they remain compliant while providing a safe, welcoming environment for their communities.

The list below lists each state's link to its laws. If you are reading this book in digital form, click on the link in the 'Website' column. If you are reading the printed book, use the address column to find the information you are looking for. I encourage your Security team to review the applicable state laws. The five crimes I listed below are the most common that Security will deal with, and knowing the elements for each will enhance the safety of the church and the professionalism of the Security team.

- Battery
- Assault
- Trespassing
- Burglary
- Theft (felony or misdemeanor)

Disclaimer: At the time this book was published, all links were thoroughly checked for accuracy. However, since the internet is constantly evolving, some links may have changed or become inactive over time. If you come across a link that no longer works or appears to be incorrect, I would greatly appreciate it if you could bring it to my attention.

If you encounter an invalid link while searching for your state's laws, a practical strategy is to input specific search terms such as *"Montana Revised Statutes,"* "current laws in Nevada," or *"Legislative laws in South Carolina"* into your preferred search engine. Additionally, visiting the official website of your state can be an effective way to locate the most accurate and up-to-date legal information.

State	Website	Address
Alabama	Alabama State Law	https://alison.legislature.state.al.us/
Alaska	Alaska State Law	https://www.akleg.gov/basis/statutes.asp
Arizona	Arizona State Law	https://www.azleg.gov/arstitle/
Arkansas	Arkansas State Law	https://arkleg.state.ar.us/ArkansasLaw
California	California State Law	https://leginfo.legislature.ca.gov/faces/codes.xhtml
Colorado	Colorado State Law	https://leg.colorado.gov/colorado-revised-statutes
Connecticut	Connecticut State Law	https://www.cga.ct.gov/current/pub/titles.htm
Delaware	Delaware State Law	https://delcode.delaware.gov/
Florida	Florida State Law	http://www.leg.state.fl.us/statutes/
Georgia	Georgia State Law	https://www.legis.ga.gov/
Hawaii	Hawaii State Law	https://portal.ehawaii.gov/government/hawaii-legislature/
Idaho	Idaho State Law	https://legislature.idaho.gov/statutesrules/idstat/
Illinois	Illinois State Law	https://www.ilga.gov/Legislation/ILCS/Chapters
Indiana	Indiana State Law	https://iga.in.gov/laws/2025/ic/titles/1
Iowa	Iowa State Law	https://www.legis.iowa.gov/law
Kansas	Kansas State Law	https://www.ksrevisor.gov/
Kentucky	Kentucky State Law	https://legislature.ky.gov/Law/Statutes/Pages/default.aspx
Louisiana	Louisiana State Law	https://www.legis.la.gov/legis/lawsearch.aspx

Maine	Maine State Law	https://legislature.maine.gov/statutes/
Maryland	Maryland State Law	https://www.mdcourts.gov/lawlib/research/gateway-to-md-law/code-rules-laws-sources
Massachusetts	Massachusetts State Law	https://malegislature.gov/Laws/GeneralLaws
Michigan	Michigan State Law	www.legislature.mi.gov/Laws/ChapterIndex
Minnesota	Minnesota State Law	https://www.revisor.mn.gov/statutes/
Mississippi	Mississippi State Laws	https://www.sos.ms.gov/communications-publications/mississippi-law
Missouri	Missouri State Law	https://www.mo.gov/government/legislative-branch/
Montana	Montana State Law	https://archive.legmt.gov/statute/
Nebraska	Nebraska State Law	https://nebraskalegislature.gov/laws/laws.php
Nevada	Nevada State Law	https://www.leg.state.nv.us/Division/Legal/LawLibrary/NRS/index.html
New Hampshire	New Hampshire State Law	https://gc.nh.gov/rsa/html/indexes/default.aspx
New Jersey	New Jersey State Law	https://nj.gov/state/dos-statutes.shtml
New Mexico	New Mexico State Law	https://www.env.nm.gov/regulatory-resources/
New York	New York State Law	https://www.nysenate.gov/legislation/laws/CONSOLIDATED
North Carolina	North Carolina State Law	https://www.ncleg.gov/Laws/GeneralStatutes
North Dakota	North Dakota State Law	https://ndlegis.gov/general-information/north-dakota-century-code/index.html
Ohio	Ohio State Law	https://codes.ohio.gov/ohio-revised-code
Oklahoma	Oklahoma State Law	https://oksenate.gov/search-statutes-constitution
Oregon	Oregon State Law	https://www.oregonlegislature.gov/bills_laws/pages/ors.aspx
Pennsylvania	Pennsylvania State Law	https://www.palegis.us/statutes
Rhode Island	Rhode Island State Law	https://www.rilegislature.gov/pages/legislation.aspx

South Carolina	South Carolina State Law	https://www.scstatehouse.gov/code/statmast.php
South Dakota	South Dakota State Law	https://sdlegislature.gov/Statutes
Tennessee	Tennessee State Law	https://www.tncourts.gov/Tennessee%20Code
Texas	Texas State Law	https://statutes.capitol.texas.gov/
Utah	Utah State Law	https://le.utah.gov/xcode/code.html
Vermont	Vermont State Law	https://legislature.vermont.gov/statutes/
Virginia	Virginia State Law	https://law.lis.virginia.gov/vacode/
Washington	Washington State Law	https://app.leg.wa.gov/rcw/
West Virginia	West Virginia Law	https://www.wvlegislature.gov/wvcodeentire.htm
Wisconsin	Wisconsin State Law	https://docs.legis.wisconsin.gov/statutes/statutes
Wyoming	Wyoming State Law	https://www.wyoleg.gov/stateStatutes/StateStatutes

Insurance implications of carrying concealed

The implications of allowing people to carry concealed in a church can vary from jurisdiction to jurisdiction. It can vary based on which insurance company you use. However, for the most part, the following can apply to every church:

1. If someone in your congregation is known to carry concealed and gets involved in a security matter in which shots are fired, you may be held liable if procedures were not followed properly or deadly force did not apply. Having conversations with weapon carriers about security protocol is crucial for everyone. This will help eliminate serious mistakes.
2. Understand what your insurance company covers and excludes. This information will help you craft policies and procedures.
3. As mentioned previously, if your church is meeting in a school, this issue may already be decided. Most

jurisdictions ban the carrying of any firearm on school property. Depending on the location, current active police officers are exempt from this ban.

Please consult with your insurance company, the building owner if you rent, and local law enforcement officials before deciding whether or not to allow concealed weapon carriers on the property.

Review the chart below, which represents responses to the locations of services. Many churches responded and told me they meet in schools. If your church is meeting in a school, the issue of allowing firearms in the church may already be decided for you. Most states do not allow firearms on school property. I highly encourage you to review your contracts with the school district you are renting from and consult with your lawyer and local law enforcement agency(s) to better understand what is legal and what is not.

Question: Describe your Church facilities.

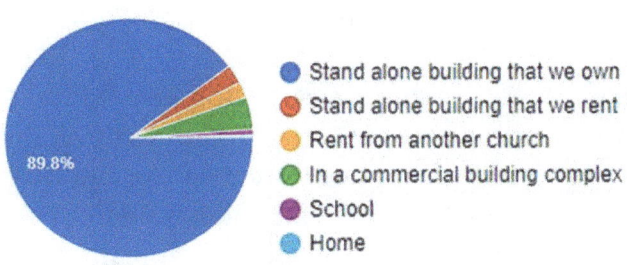

If your decision is one way or the other, that is ok. Many will agree or disagree with any direction you take so do not worry about those. Yet, if you do allow concealed firearms in your church and in particular for your security team, some issues need to be addressed:

1. Security needs to be locally trained and state-certified properly in both the use of firearms and the applicable laws. <u>Do not allow someone who has a concealed weapons permit from another state to carry while in a security role.</u> Not all states have reciprocity with each other. Local law enforcement agencies may provide this training, or reputable firearm stores/ranges may be able to assist.

   Do not put someone on the security team because they say, "I have been shooting all my life." This is similar to people saying, "I have been driving all my life." Neither statements hold up in a court of law.

2. You will need to have policies and procedures regarding firearms in the church. While it may be very difficult to know who is carrying concealed and who is not, those you know to carry need to understand that you have a security team in place and that security will handle any issues.

3. Some may recommend a secure storage area for all weapons during worship. I'm sorry, but I think this is a terrible idea. The more firearms are handled, the more likely something bad will happen. I speak from experience, having been the sergeant of all firearms training for my department for 4 ½ years with over 2,300 firearm carriers. My recommendation is this: If you allow people to carry concealed, then let it stay concealed.

4. I realize some will disagree with me on this next topic and that is ok as well. I am not a fan of open carry as I think it brings unwanted attention to a person and may make others uncomfortable. Open carrying of a firearm means that everyone can see

it. Most will wear their firearm(s) on their hip and in a holster. I have heard the counterclaims, and I understand them, but I do not open carry. In my experience, I believe the open carrying of a firearm is dangerous as it brings unnecessary attention to a person, it makes them a target for criminals, and its presence makes others who may not own guns very uncomfortable. I have spoken with my Pastor about this, and he agreed with my implementing a No Open Carry policy on church property.

Having clear policies and procedures about this will help everyone understand what is allowed and what is not.

5. Lastly, the policies need to be communicated to the congregation. How you do this is up to you. Whether you want to make an announcement or save it for small groups is your decision. However, it should be made in such a way as not to alarm your members. By communicating your decision(s), you are ensuring everyone is aware of the protocols, which limits the chances of mishaps or unintentional consequences.

The last comment on this topic is if you permit your properly trained security to carry concealed firearms on the premises, the one fast rule is that there are no exhibiting firearms to each other, no manipulation of any firearms while on the property, and no loading or unloading of the firearms. All firearms need to be carried concealed and holstered properly. Holstered properly means there is some level of retention to the holster, the trigger is covered, and the firearm is not protruding out of any clothing. Trust me on this: the more one manipulates a handgun, the greater the chance of an accident occurring. If you have a security person who is constantly fiddling with the firearm, please remove him or her from the security team immediately.

What is your position on firearms inside the church?
This is such an important topic to review with the leader(s) of any church. This should be thought out carefully while reviewing your state laws.

Some states make it illegal to bring firearms into a place of worship. In Nevada, under *Nevada Revised Statutes 202.3673* and *Nevada Administrative Code 202.020* (**Nevada Concealed Weapons Law**), the law states that a person <u>cannot</u> bring a concealed weapon into:

1. Any facility of a law enforcement agency;
2. A prison, county or city jail, or detention facility;
3. A courthouse or courtroom;
4. Any facility of a public, private school, or day care
5. Any facility of a vocational or technical school, or the Nevada System of Higher Education;
6. Any other building owned or occupied by the Federal Government, the State, or a local government; or
7. Any other place in which the carrying of a concealed firearm is prohibited by state or federal law.

It does not mention places of worship specifically, but it does mention private schools. If your place of worship also operates a school, at any level, weapons would not be permitted inside the building or even in the parking lots. It is very common for start-up churches to begin meeting in local schools. If this is the case, then no weapons are allowed on the property. Depending on your area, you are encouraged to meet with and discuss this with either the school district or the principal of that school to discuss the laws and regulations.

The exception to having guns on school property would be the full-time commissioned law enforcement officers and even some specialized firefighters who make arrests (arson investigators).

But be careful with this. Usually, this only applies to those who are present for official duties.

Nebraska has taken a different route and, through Nebraska Revised Statutes 28-1202.01, forbids the carrying of concealed weapons in a church unless certain requirements are met.

Others, like Florida and Texas, recently changed the law to allow concealed firearms in some of these places. You are encouraged to review your laws to ensure compliance. Yet, understand this: Any business, including places of worship, can ban the entry of firearms. At these places, if a person refuses to disarm himself and refuses to leave, trespass would be the normal criminal charge.

I encourage you to find your state laws and learn what is legal and illegal about firearms.

In all the churches I have attended regularly or spoken at while visiting, I have met with the Pastor(s) to discuss my authorization to carry a concealed weapon and ask them for their opinions. In every instance, the pastor(s) have had no issues with the topic, and some have even encouraged the continuation of carrying a concealed weapon. Most commissioned police officers are authorized to carry weapons off duty, and some departments recommend it while others mandate it. Officers who have honorably retired after 15 years of service are authorized to carry concealed under the *Law Enforcement Officers Safety Act of 2004* (https://www.congress.gov/bill/108th-congress/house-bill/218) This law is effective nationwide, yet it specifically states it is not intended to supersede state laws. Persons under this law, while not having to go through the normal state permitting process, if applicable, still will need to follow local and state laws in which they are living or visiting.

For those states allowing open carry, the same discussions need to take place with the leadership of the church. Are you going to allow people to open carry while in church?

There are volumes of literature and websites discussing the pros and cons of open carry, which is beyond the scope of this book. However, you will have people attend who are or who may want to open carry. If you are meeting in a school, the discussion is over, and most responsible gun owners know this. However, if you are renting a storefront or are in an established stand-alone building, people will try. Having an established policy makes enforcing of the rule feel less personal to people who want to attend and carry.

Please have discussions with your pastor and the leadership team, and please make sure everyone on the security team is aware of the protocols and speaking points if this situation arises. Dealing with a person who is adamant about carrying a firearm into the church is not the time to make up procedures as you go, you have to have plans in place prior. By having written procedures in place from the beginning, potentially long-drawn-out conversations or conflicts can be avoided.

The decision to allow church members and/or visitors to bring in firearms is neither difficult nor easy, depending on your personal beliefs about firearms.

However, legal considerations, the needs of the church, and how your congregants view this topic all need to be measured.

What is the feeling of your Congregation about having weapons in place of worship? Some places in the U.S. encourage the carrying of firearms, while others are opposed to it. Some feel having firearms in a place of worship conflicts with the nonviolent beliefs of their faith, while others feel both go hand in hand.

The chart on the next page shows the responses to the survey conducted by *Protection With Grace, LLC*, from churches nationwide.

Question: Do you allow attendees to carry firearms while attending services?

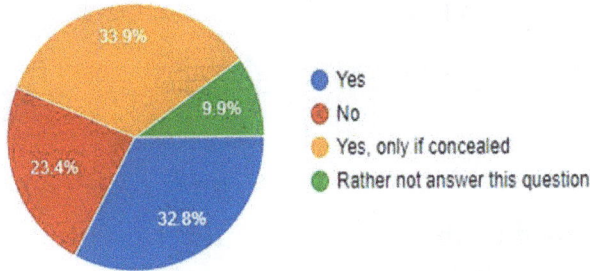

Chapter Six
PROTOCOLS

Importance of written protocols for church security

I have noted many times in this book about the necessity of having written protocols. Having written protocols for church security is crucial for ensuring that everyone involved in the security team is on the same page and knows what to do in case of an emergency. I once spoke with a pastor who was adamant against anything written down and told me it would be worse if I had one, and then something went wrong. I reminded him that things will go wrong if there is no standard, no correct way of doing something, if it is not formalized. I added that with protocols in place, those who are not adhering to them can be let go before an event (interaction with others or a major event) ever occurs. Protocols are also essential for legal compliance, financial accountability, internal communication, risk management, conflict resolution, regulatory compliance, grant applications, and fundraising for the church or particular ministries. They contribute to the church's overall health, transparency, and effectiveness in its operations.

Here are some reasons why written protocols are important:

Clarity: Written protocols clarify the roles, responsibilities, and expectations of each security team member. This helps to avoid confusion and misunderstandings, especially in high-pressure situations.

Consistency: Written protocols ensure that everyone follows the same procedures and protocols consistently, which helps to maintain safety and security standards.

Accountability: Having written protocols in place makes it easier to hold individuals accountable for their actions or inactions in case of an emergency or security breach.

Training: Written protocols provide a framework for training new security team members, ensuring that they receive consistent and comprehensive training.

Legal protection: Written protocols can provide legal protection for the church and its security team in case of any legal disputes that may arise from security incidents.

Overall, written protocols for church security are essential for ensuring that the security team is well-prepared and effective in maintaining the safety and security of the church and its members.

Written protocols should include some of the necessities for any security team to easily understand and follow. Let's review some of the basics:

1. **Designation of Documenting**
   The Security Supervisor should designate specific individuals, such as security team members or ushers, to receive and record incident reports. If someone is unable to properly complete a report form, security may assist with its completion as long as that assistance is documented as well. The Security supervisor will encourage a culture of reporting by assuring confidentiality and non-punitive measures for those who come forward.

2. **Incident Categories**

   Incidents, based on their nature, such as medical emergencies, suspicious activities, disruptive behavior, theft, and vandalism, are included in having proper documentation. If actual crimes have been committed or are being reported, it is recommended to use the forms provided by the local law enforcement or fire/paramedic agencies. Copies of those reports are usually available upon request.

3. **Incident Report Form**

   Security should be able to set up an incident report form that is conducive to your current form templates.

The Security Supervisor should make incident report forms easily accessible (digital and printed) to relevant personnel and train them to fill them out. If you are not sure where to start, visit www.protectionwithgrace.com and download a template that can be modified to fit your needs.

I recommend leaving an official space on this form for the security supervisor and the church's leadership to make comments if needed.

Writing Reports
Security leaders will train security team members and staff on how to respond appropriately to different types of incidents. The Security supervisor and the security members will determine when a report is to be taken and when not to take a report. Your decision will be needed when setting this up. In my experience, three things can happen:

1) Security takes a report for every little thing that upsets people
2) Security never takes a report that upsets leadership
3) Security is not sure when to take a report, and looks foolish.

A written protocol for when a report should be completed will make your team look more professional and free up time to work on other items.

It is important to have clear and objective language. Reports should be factual and avoid personal opinions or assumptions.

> ***Learning concept – **What you write, will be read by someone.**

Focus on the "who, what, when, where, and how" of the incident. The concept of 'using plain language' cannot be over-emphasized. I have seen reports that have been so overwhelming with big words or had so many minor details brought up that the report becomes confusing. It is best to use simple but well-defined and descriptive terms. The lack of abiding by the use of simple yet concise and descriptive narratives can lead to some, without that knowledge, dismissing or not understanding the report.

Clear and simple language is best for communication. It helps people quickly understand what happened without getting lost in complex wording or unnecessary details. This makes reporting faster and more effective.

Emphasize the importance of submitting reports promptly. Timely reporting ensures that accurate details are fresh in the memory of the security personnel and others and allows for a quicker response to incidents.

Ensure that incidents are documented promptly and effectively to mitigate future potential risks. Why take a report if it only gets shoved in a file cabinet somewhere and nothing is done about it?

Take the time to read the reports. Discuss the reports with the security leader.

This will prompt ideas on why an event may have happened, how to reduce the chances of it happening again, how to make others aware of a certain person, or even how to change your security policy. Use the reports to move forward.

Maintaining Documentation

The Security supervisor will maintain a secure and organized incident log where all reported incidents are documented. The reports must be secure from those who have no authority to review the forms, as sensitive information, privacy considerations, and confidentiality issues may be included. Both hard copies and any digital reports must be kept secure. Security and church leadership will be responsible for creating and maintaining the security of reports. Whoever is asking for a copy of a report should first be authorized to have a copy. Then, that person or entity (police, insurance, attorney) will be listed on the documentation log, along with the date and time, method of delivery (in-person, mail, or email), and who gave them the information.

Stop-gap measures for protecting vital information

Ensuring the protection of important policies and documents when employees depart from an organization is crucial for several reasons. It's important to prevent the unauthorized removal of confidential information and to safeguard intellectual property from potential compromise. Additionally, minimizing the risk of fraud and ensuring operational continuity are also significant considerations in this process.

To ensure the organization's continuity and integrity, it is crucial to take steps to prevent a former leader from taking important policies and documents when they leave the church. Here are some helpful measures that can be implemented:

1. **Establish Firm Policies and Procedures:** It is crucial to have unwavering policies in place regarding the

ownership and handling of documents. Clearly state that all documents created or used in the course of their duties belong to the church and must be returned upon departure. This process also includes who has access to documents/information as well as password protocols.

2. **Document Retention Policy**: Develop a comprehensive document retention policy clearly outlining the specific duration for retaining different types of documents, while also specifying authorized access.
3. **Review Contracts and Agreements**: All employee contracts must include clauses specifying the return of documents and intellectual property to the church upon termination or voluntary departure.
4. **Backup Important Documents**: Remember to maintain secure backups of important documents and policies in a separate location or cloud storage. This is essential to ensure that a reliable copy is always available, even if physical documents are lost or removed.
5. **Follow-Up After Departure**: After an employee leaves it is imperative to conduct a rigorous review to guarantee the return of all documents and policies. Promptly follow up if any items are missing or if there are concerns about the handling of documents.

To mitigate the risk of a former employee taking important policies and documents upon departure, implementing these measures is essential for a church.

Proactive planning and clear communication are pivotal in safeguarding the organization's assets and ensuring seamless operations. These policies must be established during any onboarding process. If documents or information were stolen, please seek out legal advice for recovery.

Should your church have a policy about documenting incidents?

Yes! This goes back to the adage that *if it is not documented, it never happened.* Incidents based on their nature, such as medical emergencies, suspicious activities, disruptive behavior, theft, and vandalism, require proper documentation. If actual crimes have been committed or are being reported, it is recommended to use the forms provided by the local law enforcement or fire/paramedic agencies. Clearly outline what incidents or activities require a written report.

Written documentation is critically important in legal and operational contexts due to the often extended duration of proceedings and the inevitable turnover of personnel involved. Because cases can take years to resolve, relying solely on memory or verbal accounts can lead to inconsistencies or loss of crucial details over time. Maintaining thorough written records ensures that information remains accurate and accessible, providing a reliable reference to refresh memories or verify prior statements.

The forms or the process do not have to be difficult or time-consuming. Create standardized reporting templates that include essential elements. This may include sections for incident details, witness statements, date and time, location, description of persons involved, and any actions taken.

Protection With Grace, LLC provides a basic, editable template for you on the website. The basics of what is needed are:

> ➢ Date
> ➢ Time
> ➢ Location
> ➢ Nature of Incident
> ➢ Description of what occurred. This is the narrative portion. It is recommended a second page be created just for the continuation of the narrative portion.

- Names of those involved (Witness, Security, Suspect, Reporting person), along with contact information.
- If desired, have a space to attach or insert a picture of the suspect. This is vital for security as now they can recall prior trespassed individuals.

Training church security personnel to write effective reports is crucial for maintaining a safe and secure environment for worship and fellowship. It is important to have descriptive, objective language. Reports should be factual and avoid personal opinions or assumptions. Focus on the "who, what, when, where, and how" of the incident.

Emphasize the importance of submitting reports promptly. Timely reporting ensures that accurate details are fresh in the memory of the security personnel and others and allows for a quicker response to incidents.

Depending on the size of your church, you may want to institute a mandatory review and analysis of the documentation of incident reports. Security should regularly review incident reports and logs to identify patterns or trends that may require attention or additional security measures.

The importance of the review and analysis is to assist with identifying potential problems, improving safety protocols, and refining emergency response protocols if necessary.

There is a major point to cover in this section about report writing or documenting incidents. Everything written must be protected from prying eyes and those who have no business reading these reports.

The reports must be secure from those who have no authority to review the forms, as sensitive information, privacy considerations, and confidentiality issues may be included.

Both hard copies and any digital reports must be kept secure. Ensure that security personnel understand the legal and ethical considerations related to report writing. This includes issues such as privacy, confidentiality, and the proper handling of sensitive information.

Why should churches have cash management controls?

Time and time again, I have spoken with strangers who ask the church for money. They almost say the same thing: "Anything will help". Most are just people honestly looking for some temporary assistance, while others have more nefarious intentions, such as where the money is kept and what type of security is involved, etc. Our church has a policy stating we do not hand cash over to anyone who is not an established member. If someone needs gas to get home, we take them to the gas station.

If someone needs money for food, we have food on hand to give to them. We invite them back on other days when food is being given out as well.

Hebrews 13:16 says, "Don't forget to do good and to share what you have because God is pleased with these kinds of sacrifices."

I agree with this 100%. This is a foundation of the church, and we should help the poor and needy. However, we are stewards of whatever God blesses us with, and those blessings are meant to further God's word and not the will of people who will take advantage of our faith.

Churches should have wise cash management controls in place for several important reasons, including financial stewardship, accountability, data accuracy, and security. Here are the key reasons why cash management controls are essential for churches:

1. Financial Stewardship: churches are entrusted with the voluntary financial contributions of their members and supporters. Effective cash management controls help ensure that these funds are used wisely, responsibly, and under the church's vision, mission, and goals.
2. Accountability: Cash management controls establish a framework for accountability within the church's financial operations. They help ensure that financial transactions are properly documented and that those responsible for handling cash are held accountable for their actions.
3. Data Accuracy: Preventing the theft of church financial resources dictates that there must be various precautions that can prevent and detect loss. If your church decides to have cash readily available for handouts, consider the following when establishing money-handling procedures:

All cash must be stored in a locked safe. Limit the number of people who have access, but assign two people to this responsibility at a minimum.

If the safe has a code, only a few should know what that code is. When one of those people leaves, the code must be changed. If the safe is opened by a key, only those whom the church has identified should have that key. Keys should be numbered, marked "Do Not Duplicate", and assigned to your volunteers or staff.

Identify those who are authorized to hand out cash. It is better to have at least two people involved with this process.

They should be vetted by the church, and just as important, be trained on how the process works. The vetting process can include interviews, training, and continuous oversight. Those handling cash must understand the protocols for receiving and distributing money. Educating them on the church's financial policies will help cement the training as well.

All transactions must be documented. I strongly recommend that this documentation include:

Time and Date

How much money was taken out

Who withdrew funds? (Remember, two people should be involved.)

Who was the person or persons receiving the funds, and a brief explanation on the ledger? (Discussed more below)

At least two people should conduct regular audits and update your members regularly about the church's financial health. This will add transparency and trust.

4. Prevention of Fraud: churches can be vulnerable to fraud or embezzlement, especially when handling cash donations. Cash management controls, such as segregation of duties and regular audits, reduce the risk of internal fraud and misappropriation of funds. This will also assist in identifying those who request money multiple times.
5. Whether you have a security present or not is up to you, but it never hurts to have another present when handing someone cash.

As mentioned above, it is important to document who the money was given to and why. It is not uncommon for scammers to continuously go back to businesses or places of worship that helped in the past, asking for additional assistance without exercising conscientious boundaries.

I am not aware of many churches that can just hand over cash to whomever; however, if you do, please think about this process more carefully. In a perfect world, only a few members of your church would be authorized to hand out money. If you have numerous members with access to money, you run the risk of handing out money to a person who was given money by someone else last week.

Finally, cash management controls are essential for churches to demonstrate financial stewardship, accountability, data accuracy, and security of the resources entrusted to them. These controls not only protect the church from financial risks but also contribute to its long-term sustainability and credibility within the community and among its members.

How can a small church ensure continuity of business?

A House of Worship serves various purposes, including worship, counseling, and spiritual growth, helping individuals deepen their faith. It's vital to have a comprehensive business plan for churches that extends beyond financial stability. This plan should ensure the smooth operation of activities and services. Here are a few examples of what churches can do to maintain business continuity:

1. Leadership Succession Planning: Identify and nurture potential successors for key positions such as Pastors, Elders, and administrative roles to guarantee a seamless leadership transition in case of resignations, retirements, or terminations.

2. Financial Sustainability: Keep thorough financial records and budgets. Broaden income sources through fundraising events and community outreach programs. Create a strong financial reserve for emergencies.

3. Volunteer Development: Cultivating a team of dedicated and skilled individuals to offer essential support for

various church activities necessitates investing in the training and growth of volunteers.

4. Cross-training: Encourage staff and volunteer cross-training. This involves providing opportunities for individuals to learn about and assist with tasks beyond their primary role. Cross-training creates safeguards by ensuring that more than one person is familiar with essential tasks, thereby reducing the impact of a key person's departure.

5. Technology and Communication: Leverage technology for communication and administration. Keep your website and social media up to date for outreach and community engagement. Utilize digital tools for managing member information and communication.

6. Regular Evaluation and Planning: Conduct periodic evaluations and audits of church activities and strategies. Use feedback from members and stakeholders to adjust plans and ensure alignment with the church's mission and vision.

Always remember that having procedures in place to ensure business continuity is crucial. Every business or House of Worship should embrace these fundamental measures.

Chapter Seven
INCIDENTS

How do you handle a disruptive church member/visitor?

Notice that the above question does not involve someone committing a crime. It addresses disruptive behavior. Security response to crimes will be covered in another section. So, the big question is, how does security handle a disruptive church member or a visitor? Unfortunately, the answer falls into the massive cauldron of "Depends." It depends on the situation, the location, who, and what is involved. The 'what ifs' of this topic are endless but let's discuss some basic principles that will hopefully keep the church, the security team, the congregants, and yes, even the disrupter safe.

As mentioned in the introduction of this book, *Protection With Grace LLC* was founded on the principle that all people will be treated with respect. While some people will need to be escorted off the property, arrested by law enforcement, or directed to counseling, it will all be based on grace. This means that no overreaction, bullying, belittling, or unnecessary force can be used - period.

Disruptive behavior is any behavior that is disrespectful to the solemnity of worship. It can include talking loudly, yelling, running around with no purpose, playing music, harassing others, using electronic devices, being under the influence of alcohol or drugs, and eating or drinking during service. It can include inappropriate dress as well.

I have seen churches hand visitors small blankets to wrap themselves in or place on their laps while visiting.

This is the grace part – instead of refusing entry or belittling someone for wearing what the church considers inappropriate, it is better to discreetly help them understand the protocols of the church and allow them to temporarily conform to the dress code of the church.

Disrespectful language and behavior are a bit more intentional than the above examples and may need to be addressed faster. I once observed a residentially challenged person enter the church, and at first, he sat down and appeared to be following along with the happenings in the sanctuary. However, within a few minutes, he began to pace back and forth in the back and then exited into the foyer. I asked him if he was ok, and he immediately started yelling and swearing loudly. He was escorted out very fast. And now the grace part – once outside, I again asked him if he was ok or if he needed medical attention. He showed me he was not interested in my line of questioning or concern and told me, in no uncertain terms, that he was going to whoop me. As discussed earlier about how security should act, I gave him no indication I was interested in a fight (but kept my distance for safety purposes) and by lowering my voice and demeanor, the situation was diffused. As I was trespassing him from the property, he walked away, still cussing at me and waving hand gestures to me, but nothing more.

Honestly, I did not know what he was dealing with and had no information on his past. People have the right to be angry, but that does not give us the right to belittle them or escalate a situation. We do have an obligation to protect others. In the above situation, he might have felt he won that 'battle', but the truth is, we all did, as everyone went home safely.

Disruptive people in a place of worship can be frustrating to security. Unless there is an actual crime being committed, approach the person in a calm and non-threatening manner and in a low voice or hushed tone, ask him/her if they are ok.

By doing so, you are communicating to the person you would rather help than hurt. Once you ask them, listen. I firmly believe most people just want to be heard.

Throughout my law enforcement career, I have been to countless calls for service where people just wanted to vent or feel that someone was hearing what they were saying. Sometimes the problem was not rectified but they were left knowing that at least someone heard them and acknowledged what they were saying. The same applies to disruptive people in places of worship. Listen to what they are saying as long as it is not making others uncomfortable and give indications you are engaged in the conversation by nodding when appropriate or asking clarifying questions. In a conflict resolution process, this equates to the idea that when we decrease our ego, our control of the situation increases.

Once the needs or wants of the person are communicated, be completely honest with them. Let them know what the church protocols and the expected appropriate behavior are and what will be tolerated and what won't be tolerated. Remind them they are in a place of worship and you are there to help. If they refuse any of the soft approaches you are trying, then that person needs to be escorted off the property. I recommend having others with you just in case the person wants to increase the disruptiveness or is giving indications the situation is about to become physical. *(Having the congregants engage to help is discussed below.)*

If the unruly person leaves the building after the disturbance, a security team member will follow the person until they leave the property, without irritating, interrupting, blocking the path of, or engaging in threatening conversations with the person. Security will note any descriptors of the person(s) and a license plate number should be recorded, if applicable. Security will determine if the incident warrants calling law enforcement, using the emergency or non-emergency numbers.

If the unruly person leaves the building but remains in the parking lot, and law enforcement has been called, the security team will continue to observe the unruly person from a distance until they depart or the police arrive. If applicable, a license plate number should be recorded.

If a person causes a disturbance and refuses to leave the premises, the security team members should contact the police. The unruly person should be given the option to leave, provided no other crimes have been committed, and observed until they depart the premises or until the police arrive. If the unruly person departs, any descriptors of the person(s) should be noted, and a license plate number should be recorded, if applicable. If the person refuses to leave the building, security should call 9-1-1 immediately. Security will continue to request the person to leave while ensuring the person does not access any other part of the building. Depending on the type of threat and/or at the judgment of the Pastor, with consultation from the Security Supervisor, evacuation of the church may be necessary.

The church I attend is very good about feeding the residentially challenged and giving them relief during the blistering summer months in Las Vegas, and, believe it or not, during the cold winter months.

For the most part, all behave as expected from anyone else.

However, there was one young man who increasingly tried to push the limit every time he showed up. On Sunday morning, he came to the front door and tried to push his way in. I saw that he was under the influence of a narcotic, and his behavior was erratic.

I let my other security members know, and we immediately blocked his entrance. We told him we would bring food and coffee out to him (which was the norm for him), but he was adamant about wanting to come in.

We calmly told him no and, using good body positioning, were able to move him from the door and away from people wanting to come in. He became agitated and began to throw fake punches at us, indicating he was going to fight us.

Luckily for all of us, my security partner, who is also a retired law enforcement officer, and I were not taking the bait, and we both knew the feinting of the punches and the attempted kicks were nothing more than showmanship. He then suddenly stopped his aggressive behavior and walked off. **Just like that!** My partner and I looked at each other and as we turned around, we saw three other men from the church standing behind us. They were prepared to assist if needed but they knew, based on prior communication with them, to let security handle these types of circumstances.

Handling disruptive people, be they church members or visitors, dictates a sensitive and well-thought-out approach. The safety of the congregants and staff, as well as that of the disruptive person, must be considered. All need to be treated with dignity and empathy.

Proverbs 14:31 Whoever oppresses the poor shows contempt for their Maker, but whoever is kind to the needy honors God.

Security needs to be trained not to overreact and should be well-versed in conflict resolution techniques, as taught by *Protection With Grace*. Even more importantly, the policies and procedures your leadership team devised need to be implemented fairly to all and must be consistent. This will further reduce your chances of being accused of any type of discrimination.

Overreacting to a situation tends to increase the need to use some type of force (pushing and shoving, handcuffing, loud shouts, commands, the list goes on). Hopefully, now you understand the importance of assigning the right people to a security team. church security should be trained or have experience in conflict resolution and de-escalation techniques to calmly resolve most situations.

Your church should have a well-drafted protocol about when to put your hands on a disruptive person. This needs to follow your state law and should be reviewed by your local law enforcement agency.

Encouraging the quick use of putting hands on people who may be disruptive will lead to lawsuits and, more importantly, people getting hurt. Remember, the church is not there to hurt people, and security needs to be on board with this concept. Church security should not be a proving ground for those wishing to work in security somewhere else in the future.

As this book repeatedly states, the best security response is one that no one hears about. It would have been very easy for me to engage both people mentioned above and increase the response or force, but why? Why intentionally aggravate a situation when it is not needed? Why intentionally create more disharmony and mistrust of the church? We have to remember who we work for in these situations, and it is not the Pastor.

What God's Word says about the use of force

Here are some realities to consider about physical contact when drafting a security policy and procedure guide:

1. In my experience, no one likes physical confrontation. When this happens, almost everyone involved ends up being injured.
2. Using force always looks bad. The moment security puts their hands on someone, there will be a person filming it. If you have an untrained security team, it will only make matters worse. However, if you have a properly trained and knowledgeable team, the actual filming will help to fend off frivolous complaints or ploys to obtain money from the church. Police have found there to be fewer complaints when officers, while using force, utilize body cameras compared to those who do not.
3. You and your leadership/elder team need to address going hands-on with someone. As mentioned above, while it never looks good, common sense tells us that sometimes it is needed. You will need to decide when and how security will intervene with physical force.

In my opinion, the Bible does not give us clear guidance on the use of force; it does give us examples of the application of force. Proverbs 24:11-12 shows us we have a responsibility to protect and defend others. John 15:13 states, *"Greater love has no one than this: to lay down one's life for one's friends."*. According to the Bible, it also says we need to turn the other cheek in Matthew 5:39. In Romans 12:17-21, we are not to repay evil with evil. These two ends of the spectrum are not contradictory if understood within the context it was meant to be. Security should show empathy and grace when safe to do so; yet they also need to act quickly and decisively when needed.

Sometimes, security has to put their hands on people
Church security teams need proper training and guidelines on the appropriate use of force. While physical intervention may be necessary in some situations, it should only be used as a last resort to protect the safety and well-being of the congregation.

Any physical contact should be minimal and nonviolent, and security personnel should only use the level of force necessary to control the situation and prevent harm. Church security personnel need to be calm, respectful, and professional in all situations and follow established protocols for handling disruptive or potentially dangerous individuals.

Each state has laws on when and to what extent security officers can use force against others (in defense). I encourage you to review your state laws on this topic.

I have made a point not to use this book as a guide for the use of force, defensive tactics, or deadly force. The training for these topics is beyond the scope of this book. I repeat what I said, no good person wants to use any type of force, but sometimes it may be needed. There are only three things to consider when deciding to use force:

>1) Security should never use physical force unless necessary,
>
>2) Security should never escalate a situation to the point where physical force is needed, and
>
>3) Security should only use the amount of force that is necessary to stop the illegal or harmful action.

It is imperative that you read and understand the laws of your state regarding what security is and what they are allowed to do in the performance of their duties.

In my state, Nevada Revised Statute NRS648.016 clearly defines what a security officer is, and believe me, it does not pertain to a volunteer security member at a church. (See the guide at the end of the book to access your state laws.)

The Bible teaches us to respect human life, and people need to be protected. Using force to protect ourselves (self-defense) or protecting others may be appropriate. Yet, your security needs to understand it is preferred that peaceful means and compassion need to be considered in all interactions.

The best use of force is the one that never happens. Earlier in the book, I mentioned the importance of placing the right people in security. Through maturity, experience, and reasoning, most problems can be resolved without anyone ever knowing they occurred.

I am a firm believer in de-escalation techniques. These techniques are strategies and communication skills used to defuse tense or potentially volatile situations. Notice here, I did not say active or ongoing violent situations. That will be covered later. De-escalation techniques aim to reduce aggression, hostility, or emotional intensity to create a safer and more manageable environment. Here are some common de-escalation techniques that you can address with your security team and employees of the church:

1. Stay calm: Maintain a calm and composed demeanor. Your calmness can have a positive influence on others and help prevent the situation from escalating further. This includes speaking in a calm and gentle tone. Avoid raising your voice, as it may escalate the situation. The best way to remain calm and be aware of your surroundings is to breathe deeply. This oxygenates the brain, allowing it to function properly. Think about a gymnast, a diver, a track and field athlete, a basketball player, etc., they all take deep breaths before their event. The same principle applies here. Those who have never experienced a critical

incident tend to have fast and shallow breaths while involved in a situation. This does not help their response.
2. Learn their name. By using a person's name while interacting with them, you are making a connection with them on a human level.
3. Control your ego: Refrain from engaging in arguments or power struggles. Do not let your ego get in the way of a peaceful resolution. Employ calming and reassuring phrases, such as "I understand," "Let's work this out together," or "I'm here to help." I have found, based on my experience, if I start with a question in the arena of: "Are you ok?" or "Do you need medical assistance?", it seems to defuse many potentially bad situations. Instead of agitating a person or putting them in a position in which they feel they have no choice but to act out or fight, focus on finding common ground or understanding the person's perspective.
4. Active listening: Pay close attention to what the other person is saying. Demonstrate that you are listening by nodding, making eye contact, and paraphrasing their concerns. Let them talk and stop interrupting.
5. Empathy: Show empathy and understanding towards the other person's feelings and perspective. This can help build rapport and defuse tension. However, fake empathy or *"Yeah-Yeahing"* someone comes off as very phony and disrespectful - (this is a pet peeve of mine).
6. Non-confrontational body language: Maintain open and non-threatening body language. Avoid crossing your arms, maintain appropriate personal space, and use open gestures. Avoid pointing fingers at someone, touching them, or staring them down. This can be misinterpreted as a challenge, and that is not your goal.
7. Give the person space: If possible, allow the person some physical space. Crowding or invading personal space can contribute to escalation. Also, it is unsafe for you. In law

enforcement, the general rule is to stay at least six feet away. This gives you a chance to react to any sudden attacks and keeps you generally out of range of a kick. However, this cannot always be accomplished based on the environment and the church layout

8. Offer choices: Provide the person with positive options or choices whenever possible. This can give them a sense of control and may help de-escalate the situation. By providing them with the idea that the decisions are theirs, they might consider that a win and leave. If they still choose to put others in danger, then you will be in good standing if and when you have to defend yourself or others.
9. Involve Support: If necessary, involve a supervisor, security personnel, or other appropriate authorities to provide additional support and assistance. I spoke earlier of asking other church members to at least stand behind you as a show of support while you or other security members handle a situation. This wall of people is a great deterrent for those who want to make a scene.
10. However, removing those who are not involved in the disturbance is sometimes more beneficial. It takes away the person's audience, keeps others safe, and allows responding police to quickly determine the location and identify who is involved.

It's important to note that de-escalation techniques may vary based on the specific context and individuals involved. Training in conflict resolution and de-escalation can be beneficial for individuals working in professions where they may encounter challenging situations regularly, such as law enforcement, healthcare, or customer service.

Years ago, while working at the police department, I was on the phone with a resident in my jurisdiction. She was elderly and she called me to voice some concerns about how the police were responding to events in her neighborhood. This was a lengthy conversation and, unfortunately, I felt it was dragging on. At one point, she paused and asked if I was still on the phone. I replied I was and that I had heard what she was saying. She became very authoritative, and she said she was more interested in the fact that I was listening to her complaints. I immediately understood what she was saying and told her she had my full attention.

We need to listen to people when they are causing a disturbance or acting out. There may be an underlying cause to their actions. I have taught conflict resolution techniques for decades, and they do work – with the right heart and the right attitude. Remember, it is protection with grace. church security is not a proving ground for violent or disrespectful behavior.

Active shooter

While it is difficult to discuss active shooter scenarios, it must be addressed. This highly emotional subject affects everyone in some way or another. Having a script written is good and is needed, but this is where people will instinctively react to the sound of gunfire. Some will freeze, others will run, and some will hide. And there will be those who actively move towards the gunfire and engage the suspect(s). If your staff has not reviewed the video, please take the time to review the link below, which describes what to do during an actual event.

Run-Hide-Fight
(https://www.youtube.com/watch?v=5VcSwejU2D0)

Or review the FBI's website (https://www.fbi.gov/video-repository/run-hide-fight-020824.mp4/view).

Unfortunately, 49% of the places of worship responding to the Protection With Grace, LLC survey indicated they were unaware such a video existed. Sadly, 14% of the respondents stated they were aware of the video but would not share it with the congregants or even discuss it during small group gatherings. The pie chart below shows the full response to the question:

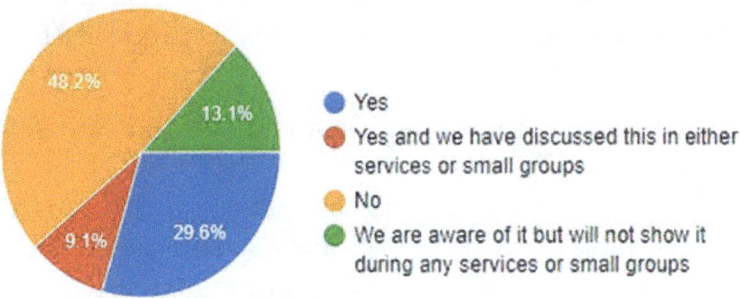

The presentations of the *Run-Hide-Fight* video should be done with care and understanding so as not to frighten but to inform. A free link can be found on the www.protectionwithgrace.com website. I encourage you and your staff to review the video first and then design a system for introducing it to your congregants. Another option is to review the **Move-Secure-Defend**(Move_Secure_Defend-8-24-22.pdf) reference guide, produced by the Idaho Office of State Board of Education. The information learned from the video, the guide, and subsequent discussions can help your congregants stay safer at work, shopping, or wherever an active shooter situation begins. Please find the time to discuss real-world situations with your congregation and have them better prepared.

A good, well-written security procedure addressing active shooters, shared with the staff and the Congregation, is vital and encouraged.

Security needs to understand their capabilities and experience in dealing with such a horrible crime. If they are armed, they should be very aggressive in stopping the person(s). If they are not armed, they need to decide whether to Run, Hide, Fight, or be able to help others.

During an active shooter situation, there really will not be time to make announcements or spend time trying to warn the Pastor – people will already know. Your security training should entail some of the following for your congregants and staff to understand before any tragedy:

1. If they can exit the building, then run out and find safe shelter elsewhere.
2. If people cannot flee the building, then find rooms in which the doors can be locked and/or barricaded. Find any items to put in front of the doors or to hold as shields. Those working in offices, classrooms, and nurseries should already be trained in how to lock and barricade their respective doors.
3. If people are unable to flee or hide, the only response should be to attack. How people do this cannot be answered, except that there is strength in numbers. All too often, we read about a gunman entering a room and the victims huddled in the corner. This is exactly what the criminals want. If cornered, the only option is to attack with everything available.

Call 9-1-1 or direct others to call. The following information should be relayed:

1. Identify yourself.
2. Advise of the crime(s) being actively committed.
3. Tell them your physical and clothing description.
4. Provide information about where the criminal is and what they are wearing.
5. Acknowledge and listen for further instructions from the dispatcher if safe to do so.

All across the nation, the police are trained in active shooter response. And their number one goal during this type of crime is to stop or eliminate the threat(s). That means, when they arrive on the scene, there is no time to assess anyone with injuries, there is no time for introductions or small talk. Their only focus is moving towards the sound of gunfire. Your security team needs to understand this and be prepared to get out of the way.

The following indicates some Do's and Don'ts for security during an active shooter situation/police response:
1. If safe to do so, holster the firearm when the cops arrive. Not all who respond will recognize all security personnel. If security exhibits a firearm, when ordered to drop their weapon, they must do so.
2. Security should not run towards the police upon arrival.
3. Have a visible ID and refrain from any sudden movements.
4. Follow the instructions given without hesitation.
5. Provide building information, layout, and/or assist with unlocking doors.
6. Having a "Go Bag" at the ready will assist first responders. The bag should contain keys to all rooms, a map of the property, and a functioning church radio.
7. If there is a surveillance room, let the police have access and operate the system for them if told.
8. Do not confront the police or disobey their commands. This can create a very dangerous situation, put more lives at risk, and delay the police's response. Now is not the time to be the hero.
9. Do not join them in their response. Once the police have identified you, they will give you orders. Please listen and adhere to them.

There is no way to simplify or whitewash the active shooter topic. It is filled with emotions, fear, and the unknown. Sometimes, we do not know why these horrific crimes occur, and sometimes, the criminals let us know, through manifestos or social media statements, the hate and fury they have for a particular group of people or just people in general.

Regardless, you have taken on the role of the leader for your place of worship. Please find a way to get the training, procedures, and readiness for your Congregation.

De-brief all incidents
During my career, debriefing incidents has always been beneficial and educational. First responders debrief incidents to self-critique and discuss what went well and what went wrong. Hearing others say you made a mistake can be difficult, but the long-term benefits can make future critical incidents much safer. While not on the scale of first responders, church security teams should get in the habit of debriefing any incident that occurs. These conversations are led by the team leader or the Director of Security. This can include injuries, accidents, crimes, and first responder activity on or near the property. During these debriefs, each member should be able to express what they saw and did during the incident. They should articulate what went well as well as what went wrong. It is important to understand that none of these conversations should be taken personally, and one should have some thick skin to avoid being offended. These conversations should also discuss if the current church security policy needs to be adjusted, if current team practices need to be reviewed, or if more training should be provided.

Debriefings after incidents help improve the team, allowing church members to feel safer and giving you, as the security leader, confidence that your response actions will continue to improve.

Be a good witness
When force is not necessary or applicable under the law, just being a witness can be just as important. Being a good witness means being aware of your surroundings and alert to potential threats.

Church members can play an important role in helping to maintain the safety and security of the congregation by being observant and reporting any suspicious behavior or activity to the church security team or local law enforcement.

This includes noting the details of any individuals or vehicles that seem out of place and any unusual behaviors or activities. It is important to encourage them to do so discreetly and without drawing attention to themselves and to avoid escalating the situation or putting themselves or others at risk. Being a good witness can help prevent potential incidents and protect the safety of the congregation.

Chapter Eight
COMMON SECURITY ISSUES

Three common issues we should not overlook
The first is domestic violence. According to the National Coalition Against Domestic Violence website, **Domestic Violence Statistics (www.thehotline.org)** states that 1 in 4 women and 1 in 9 men have been victims of domestic violence. That is quite a staggering number. Domestic violence encompasses all neighborhoods, economic statuses, education levels, and professions. And just to be clear, domestic violence does not always mean there is actual physical violence happening. It can include emotional abuse, verbal abuse, psychological abuse, financial abuse (which causes the victim to have to stay), threats, neglect, or isolation. It is essential to understand what domestic violence is in your state. There are links at www.protectionwithgrace.com to find your state's domestic violence laws.

If a staff member or congregant approaches you and tells you he or she is a victim of domestic violence, it is not your place to investigate or offer marital counseling. You actually might make the situation worse. Marital counseling requires a person to be a licensed clinical social worker or clinical psychologist.

It is important to remember that pastoral counseling requires an ordained clergyperson or chaplaincy training.

Your role is to help notify the local authorities and/or provide transportation to a shelter set up to handle domestic violence victims. The same applies to your security. Their procedures should reflect the need to communicate with you first if a crime is not being committed in front of them. If that happens, then security should notify the police immediately and assist the victim if possible.

The second issue you should not overlook is child custody disputes. These can be seen as a highly emotional situation with a tendency to become violent. If you have members who are going through a child custody case or have already been through the courts and regularly attend your church, understand that you or your security team are not the ones to enforce the court documents as to who has the child at any given time. If a dispute occurs on the property, security should notify the police immediately and then stand by. That's it. Security should not be inserting themselves into a potentially volatile situation, nor should they take sides.

Sometimes, parents who have separated and have children will still attend the same place of worship. Your responsibility is to set clear boundaries for interacting with each other while on-premises and keep you and security informed of any changes to the child custody/visitation court documents.

The third issue that you and security will need to address is the mentally ill. I have stated numerous times in this book that mental illness is not a crime, nor should it be treated as such. Trained medical and clinical behavioral professionals should treat it. With that, you and your security team need to realize that this not only pertains to the residentially challenged population you serve, but could also pertain to members of your church.

It is estimated that approximately 30% of residentially challenged people are dealing with some type/level of mental illness.

Most places of worship already know the local nonprofits that the residentially challenged can visit for food, shelter, and sometimes medical attention. But what do you do when there is someone in your congregation dealing with mental illness?

If the member or family of the member has been attending for some time, you may already be aware of the situation and have spoken with them about how to act in case there is an episode or reaction to some stimuli. The recommendation here is for your entire staff to be trained in how to approach a member in a medical crisis and how to respond in case the situation negatively affects the entire Congregation. Check with your local first responders to determine if they offer any type of crisis intervention training. This type of training will provide practical response methods for those who are contemplating suicide, someone who is having a breakdown or setback, and how to respond to someone experiencing signs of Excited Delirium.

Law enforcement agencies nationwide train to respond to and handle incidents of Excited Delirium. From the training, we have been taught that Excited Delirium is a particularly dangerous situation in which death may occur. People experiencing this are very aggressive, suffer paranoia, are in panic mode, and can become very violent. The reasons why someone might suffer from Excited Delirium are based either on some type of psychiatric illness or an illicit drug-induced reaction. Either way, that person needs medical attention immediately. Your written security protocols should include protecting others nearby, speaking slowly in a calm voice to the person, and not acting aggressively.

Those who are suffering from Excited Delirium can possess extraordinary strength, and it will take many people to detain someone until medical personnel arrive.

Because Excited Delirium affects the breathing mechanisms, understand that if security needs to use force to subdue the person, they should immediately focus on the person's breathing.

It is very easy for someone in this condition to slip into respiratory arrest, which in turn leads to cardiac arrest. Someone needs to be directly assigned to monitor only the breathing of the person until medical arrives. This person should not be assigned to anything else. Once medical and police arrive, back off and let them handle everything from there. Be prepared to provide any type of statements and videos if requested.

Churches can play a very positive role in helping those with mental illness if the staff and security are properly trained. Through education, support, referrals, and kindness, you can help improve the worship experience for those who might also suffer from stigmatization or victimization from the outside world.

Cybercrimes
On a totally but just as important level, churches need to understand the effects of cybercrimes and how to disrupt any attempts to steal church data and money. As churches and other religious organizations increasingly rely on technology to communicate and operate everyday church activities, they are also becoming more vulnerable to cyberattacks.

In my quest to obtain as many church contacts as possible to send out church security surveys, I researched numerous databases and open-source websites (Facebook®, Twitter®, Google®). What I found was very interesting. It is amazing how many churches have a personal email account as the primary contact. And when I say personal, I mean there is no mention of the church's name anywhere in the address. We know people come and go in every industry when talking about real-life human interactions and relationships. Churches are no different. It does not make sense to have one person have access to all of the church's data, records, and correspondence through a personal email account. What makes more sense is for churches of all sizes to have an official email address (with the church's name or some variant of that) when dealing with formal communications.

Yes, changing passwords when workers or volunteers come and go can be cumbersome, but what is worse is not having possession of historical communications, some of which may be sensitive.

The last point on this topic is if a worker or volunteer is allowed to use a personal email to conduct church business and they leave, that means you lose all the contacts as well.

What does this mean for the church? All communication about congregants' health issues, family issues, church issues, financial statements, work performance evaluations, and any disciplinary actions is now out of the church's control and stored somewhere else. Yes, you can ask for the information to be deleted and/or returned, but there is no way you can be sure of this occurring.

People will say the same can happen even if someone has a church email account, which is true. However, a firm policy about only using church emails for church business will protect you in case information is inadvertently sent out. This policy can also be included in your onboarding process for new employees or volunteers.

The recommendation is that two members of the church should have access to the email system. It depends on your place of worship and your business model on who that will be, but if one person leaves (for whatever reason), the church still can function properly with no setbacks. If a person does leave on their own or is asked to leave, access to their church-authorized email address is immediately blocked.

Who has the passwords?
Limiting the number of people who have passwords is one way to reduce the risk of cyber theft, but it should not be the only solution.

Here are some additional measures that can help prevent cyber theft:

> Implement a firm password policy: Require employees to create strong passwords that are at least 12 characters long and include a combination of letters, numbers, and special characters.
>
> Encourage employees to use password managers to store and manage their passwords securely. Most institutions and companies want passwords to be changed periodically. You can incorporate the same requirement for your staff.

Other considerations
Depending on the size of the church and the budget, you may want to use multi-factor authentication:
> Multi-factor authentication adds an extra layer of security to your login process, making it more difficult for hackers to gain access to your accounts. You can use authentication methods such as biometrics, SMS codes, or security keys.

Regularly update software and systems: Make sure that all software and systems are up to date with the latest security patches and updates. This will help prevent hackers from exploiting known vulnerabilities.

Train employees, including your security team, on cybersecurity best practices: Educate employees/volunteers on how to identify and avoid phishing scams, suspicious emails, and social engineering tactics.

Your staff and your security should always be monitoring for suspicious activity. Any time a scam or suspicious message is received, the entire staff needs to be aware of it.

Ask you staff to not be overcome with embarrassment and hide the fact they have been or might have been a victim of a cybercrime.

In order to maintain data security and protect sensitive information, it is crucial to restrict employee access to data. To do so, it is recommended to develop a computer access hierarchy that outlines the specific data sets that each employee is authorized to access based on their job responsibilities. This approach ensures that employees only have access to the information necessary to effectively perform their job functions, while also minimizing the risk of data breaches and misuse of information.

Using any of the above suggestions, you can help prevent cyber theft and protect your organization's sensitive data, including that of your members.

Protection measures for tithing and offerings
With tithes or offerings coming into the church, whether it is through online donations or the traditional in-house method, having security protocols in place will help ensure the money is collected and deposited safely.

But before we move on, I would like to reiterate a personal opinion—I do not believe security should be involved in collecting, depositing, and auditing the monies. When a security person is busy passing the plate or counting the money, they are not doing what security is supposed to do—watch over everything. If you have a small church, then individuals might be assigned numerous roles, and I understand that. This is just something to think about as your church grows and expands.

Another aspect to consider is not having married couples count on the same Sunday. This situation could create the appearance of favoritism or a potential conflict of interest.

The prevention of financial discrepancies is stronger when two individuals handle the counting. When married couples count, they are looked at as a single entity and not as separate.

First, with the online system, using a reputable payment gateway will help eliminate unknown charges or fees and can assist with safeguarding all transactions. The *Payment Card Industry Data Security Standard (PCI DSS)* is a good place to start. Their goal is to protect the security of sensitive cardholder information (card numbers, CV numbers, and expiration dates).

If you can, encrypt your website with a Secure Sockets Layer (SSL). This helps protect any data transmitted, including financial information, from being intercepted by malicious parties.

No matter what system you have in place, you will need to have regular audits. By conducting regular security audits of the church website and online payment system to identify and address any vulnerabilities or weaknesses, you are showing due diligence.

Hiring a third-party security expert to perform penetration testing and code reviews may be needed if a problem does arise. Let your members know the steps you have taken to safeguard their private information. If you can clearly outline the church's private policy regarding the collection and use of donor information, you will give them confidence in knowing their donations are being wisely utilized. You can also set up a communication system in which donors are being educated about potential new scams and who to contact in case they have been asked to donate to another site.

Another factor to consider about online tithing is that you can establish alerts for suspicious activity or unusual patterns. You should be considering a backup and disaster recovery system to ensure that donor data remains accessible and protected in the event of a security breach or failure.

Second, no church is too small not to have collection and deposit protocols in place. To ensure the security of collected donations and their safe deposit, a church can take certain steps when collecting traditional tithes and offerings. The first step is to establish a secure collection process. This can be done by assigning trusted and vetted individuals or a designated team to handle the collection.

They should use tamper-evident bags or lockable containers to store cash and checks securely. Even with a team, one person should be overseeing the entire collection process. Implementing a dual custody approach will help. Two members should be required to handle (count and sort) and then transport the collected funds. This reduces the risk of theft or mishandling, thus guaranteeing accountability.

To ensure timely and secure handling of the offerings, it is recommended to deposit them into the church's bank account as soon as possible after collection, ideally on the same day.
This will help to maintain accurate financial records and prevent any potential risks associated with storing cash on-site.

When transporting donations to the bank, it's crucial to ensure the safety and security of the funds. To achieve this, it's recommended to use a secure and discreet method of transportation. For instance, you may consider using a locked cash bag or a vehicle with secure storage compartments. These will prevent unauthorized access to the donations during transit. In addition, it's essential to avoid predictable patterns or routines that could make the church vulnerable to theft. For example, you could vary the time and route of transportation regularly.

This will make it difficult for potential thieves to predict when and where the donations will be transported.

Lastly, it's advisable to ensure that the individuals responsible for transportation are trustworthy and reliable. They should be aware of the importance of maintaining confidentiality and should be trained in handling the donations securely.

By following these guidelines, you can help to safeguard the donations and protect the church from theft or fraud.

Establishing clear and concise procedures for depositing funds in collaboration with the bank is imperative. Such procedures may include utilizing night deposit boxes or arranging for armored car services for larger deposits.

Adhere to the bank's guidelines for handling cash deposits and ensure that all deposits are adequately documented. This will ensure that financial resources are appropriately managed and that deposits are secure.

As for record-keeping, it is crucial to maintain a comprehensive and accurate record of all donations collected. The record should include the date, amount, and source of each contribution. It is also vital to implement checks and balances to ensure that the deposited amounts match the recorded totals. This measure is necessary to detect any discrepancies that may arise and promptly investigate them.

Keep in mind that maintaining accurate records and implementing adequate checks and balances will help build trust with donors, ensure compliance with legal requirements, and enable effective management of the organization's finances.

It is important to establish internal controls to prevent and detect fraud. This can be done by segregating duties, conducting regular reconciliations, and implementing oversight mechanisms.

Encouraging transparency and accountability among staff and volunteers involved in handling the church's finances can also help prevent fraud.

Security measures need to be thought out and implemented to protect the collected offerings and prevent any unauthorized access or theft. It is recommended to install security cameras and audible alarms in the areas where these items are stored. This will not only deter potential thieves but also help in identifying them in the event of a break-in. Additionally, to further strengthen the security measures, access to sensitive areas where offerings are kept should be strictly limited to authorized personnel only. This will ensure that only those who have been granted access can enter the area, reducing the risk of theft or misuse of offerings. By implementing these security measures, you can help keep your valuable items secure and protect against potential losses.

It is imperative to encourage comprehensive training for the staff and volunteers on proper cash handling procedures, security protocols, and fraud prevention measures. It is also crucial to educate them about the significance of safeguarding donations and adhering to established policies and controls. Such training not only ensures the safety of organizational funds but also strengthens its credibility and trustworthiness in the community. Training should be made a mandatory part of the onboarding process, and refresher courses should be conducted periodically to reinforce the knowledge and skills acquired. Please consider obtaining insurance coverage for potential losses resulting from theft, robbery, or any other unforeseen events.

Seeking the advice of an insurance provider to assess the church's risk exposure and to determine the appropriate coverage options is paramount. Doing so would enable the church to stay protected against unforeseen circumstances.

The implementation of the above recommendations can significantly enhance the security of collected tithes and offerings, thus ensuring the safety of these donations and their subsequent deposit into the church's bank account. These measures may include the adoption of a secure collection system, the use of tamper-proof bags or containers, and the involvement of multiple individuals in the counting and depositing of the funds. Adherence to these guidelines serves to safeguard the integrity of the donations and fosters the trust of the congregation. Furthermore, the accurate recording and documentation of all transactions are imperative to ensure transparency and accountability to the Congregation.

Accidents

Accidents can happen anywhere, and worship spaces are no exception. In fact, everyday incidents during services occur just as frequently as they do in any other setting. Much of the literature on security teams for Houses of Worship tends to focus on protocols for criminal events, while only briefly mentioning health-related incidents like fainting or heart attacks. Although these medical emergencies are important, it is vital to consider the more routine mishaps that can occur within these sacred spaces.

Imagine a bustling church during a Sunday service: congregants moving about, children playing, and the elderly navigating the environment. In this lively atmosphere, slips, trips, and falls can easily happen. Someone may stumble on an uneven floor, or a child might dart into an unsuspecting adult's path, leading to a collision. If your church features a raised stage for performances or worship, the risk of a fall becomes even more pronounced during skits or dramatic presentations.

In addition, environmental factors can create hazards. In snowy regions or areas prone to heavy rainfall, the entrances and hallways can become dangerously slick, increasing the likelihood of falls. It's essential to stay vigilant about maintaining safe conditions.

Moreover, consider the parking lot — an often-overlooked area where potential accidents can occur. Drivers entering or exiting may experience unexpected medical episodes while behind the wheel. An article from the National Highway Traffic Safety Administration, titled *"The Contribution of Medical Conditions to Passenger Vehicle Crashes"*, can be found at the link below (**https://crashstats.nhtsa.dot.gov/Api/Public/ViewPublication/811219**). It indicates that accidents caused by such medical conditions are rare, making up only 1.3% of all vehicle crashes. However, the possibility remains, especially as drivers age and their health conditions may deteriorate.

While criminal incidents warrant attention, it is equally important to account for the everyday risks that can arise during worship and in the surrounding areas. If we are aware of possible hazards, we can create a safer environment for all who gather in our places of worship.

Events
Places of worship often organize a diverse array of events throughout the year, each bringing unique challenges and opportunities. It is vital that Security participates in the event planning process.

Involving security teams in discussions and meetings regarding the agenda and activities is essential.
It is counterproductive to keep critical information isolated from security professionals, as this can hinder their ability to craft an effective safety plan in a timely manner.

This book emphasizes the importance of including security representatives in all leadership and planning meetings, regardless of whether or not they have a formal voting role. Those with expertise in security can offer invaluable recommendations on a wide range of event or facility planning aspects. Their input can help ensure that both safety and efficiency are prioritized from the outset.

This includes guidance on optimal vehicle and pedestrian access routes, strategic placement of barriers to control crowd flow, selection of preferred vendor locations, and the arrangement of restroom facilities to enhance accessibility and safety.

Off-site events are highly encouraged for churches to reach out and engage with the community. However, such events can also heighten exposure to unfamiliar individuals, potentially increasing risks for congregation members. Therefore, it's imperative that the security team is well-versed in all the details surrounding these gatherings to effectively minimize any threats to safety.

In this book, we have deliberately refrained from discussing specific crimes to avoid distressing those who may have experienced such traumas. Nevertheless, it's important to acknowledge that a wealth of unsettling accounts and news reports regarding crimes at church events can be found online, underscoring the need for vigilant security measures in all aspects of event planning.

Waivers for trips and events
Like other organizations, churches often arrange field trips for various activities such as community service, educational experiences, or social events.

When churches organize field trips, they should ask participants to sign waivers. This shows that they take safety seriously.

Waivers allow people to understand and accept any risks involved in the trip. They also show respect for each person's ability to make their own choices.

By requiring waivers, churches confirm that everyone is aware of the potential risks and agrees to them. This not only protects the church from unexpected problems but also shows that they trust their members to make informed decisions.

Waivers are a way for the church and its members to agree that everyone is responsible for their safety. They show a strong commitment to keeping everyone safe while respecting each person's integrity and choices.

When planning a field trip or excursion with your congregants, please consider the following:

1. **Liability Protection:** A waiver is necessary to protect the church from legal liability in the event of accidents or injuries during the field trip. It acknowledges that participants are aware of and accept the potential risks involved.

2. **Informed Consent:** Before the trip, participants (or their parents if they're under 18) need to know about any risks involved. This helps them make informed choices about joining the trip.

3. **Medical Consent:** The waivers allow emergency medical treatment during the trip if someone gets hurt or sick.

4. **Insurance Requirements:** Some insurance policies need waivers. These documents help with insurance claims if something happens.

5. **Legal Documentation:** In case of a disagreement or legal action, waivers show that participants knew about the risks and agreed to them.

6. **Safety and Responsibility:** The waivers remind participants to think about their safety and what they need

to do to be safe during the trip. This makes things safer for everyone.

While waivers don't eliminate all risks or liability, they are a useful tool in managing potential legal and safety issues related to field trips. Yet, by having waivers signed and in hand, you now have a roster of participants, with emergency contact information in the event of an accident or situation in which the information is needed for communication or accountability.

When the church plans a field trip, the security team needs to know all the details, especially if kids are going. When the security team knows all about the trips, they show that they take responsibility and understand that they have to look out for the kids and everyone else. It's not just being careful but making sure everyone can trust that they'll be safe.

By letting the security team know about the trips, the church shows that it cares about everyone's safety. It understands that trips are not just for fun, but that it needs to keep an eye on everyone who goes.

The following insert is from Tim Fletcher. Yes, he is my brother. He is a Man of God and a dedicated public servant. Before his time in law enforcement, Tim ministered as a Christian Missionary to over four hundred churches across the country. He planted and pastored two churches in Newfoundland, Canada. He holds a Bachelor of Divinity, a Master of Divinity, and a Doctorate in Biblical Studies. He and his wife, Nina, are currently full-time RVers and enjoy attending new churches across the nation.

I was a missionary for ten years. I traveled the country and spoke at hundreds of churches. Once, I was scheduled to preach at an inner-city church in Philadelphia. The front doors of the church were literally on the sidewalk. As you walked through the doors, you were in the church's main sanctuary, with the pulpit at the far end. There was a chair next to the door and a large pipe wrench. It came to the point of the service where I was to speak. I started to rise, and the pastor grabbed my arm and said, "Brother, if anything happens in the back, don't you worry; you just keep preaching." This was my introduction to church security. Fast-forward a few years. I was a few years into a new career as a police officer. I was at my home church in Las Vegas, sitting in the morning service, listening to the preaching, when a friend of mine got out of his seat.

He took a couple of steps and fell to the floor. A couple of other men and I managed to get him to the hallway and call for an ambulance. He was having a medical episode.

I retired from the police department in 2020, and Nina and I have been full-time RV'ers since then. On most Saturday nights, I search websites for a church to attend. I would estimate that we have been in about two hundred churches nationwide in the last five years.

Some of those churches had twenty people in them, and others had thousands. We have been treated like royalty in some churches, and in others, no one said anything to us.

We have been greeted as we drove into the parking lot, but most times, we fend for ourselves. We have been greeted at the door and shown where to go and a few times we stood at the entrance wondering where the main service was. It is about people: the church membership, the visitors, the kids, and the staff. I know that, ultimately, it is about the Lord, but we are trying to get people to the Lord. We want to bring members closer to the Lord, introduce the unsaved to Jesus Christ, and allow the staff to serve the Lord in a safe environment.

Does your membership know that if someone has a medical problem, someone knows what to do? Has someone noticed the visitors and acknowledged them? Does your staff know that their kids are safe while they are teaching your kids?

As Nina and I visit churches around the country, we feel more comfortable in smaller churches because everyone knows everyone. When we are at bigger churches, I look for men with earpieces attached to radios. This tells me that someone is paying attention to what is going on, which makes me feel comfortable.

Church security is just as important as an air conditioner for a church in the desert or a furnace for a church in the North. If either is broken, no one will be looking for the Lord if they are sweating in the stifling heat or shivering in the icy cold.

If someone's car gets broken into, you are going to hear about it. If a computer is taken, someone is going to complain. A member has a heart attack, and no one knows what to do - that will come back to haunt you. Let the wrong person teach a Sunday school class; the consequences could be disastrous.

As you take steps toward church security and establishing emergency procedures, I encourage you to remember what Jesus said in Matthew 20:28

" The Son of man came not to be ministered unto, but to minister..."

Take care of your people and take care of each other.

Victimizations

Is your leadership team set up to recognize what child abuse or child endangerment is? Are they capable of understanding the signs of elder abuse or elder endangerment? Does anyone on your team know what spousal abuse looks like? Does your leadership team know what a mandatory reporter is and the laws on reporting abuse? If you are not sure what your role is as it pertains to your state law, please review *Clergy as Mandatory Reporters of Child Abuse and Neglect* (www.childwelfare.gov). Select your state and review the law. Also, a recommendation is to check your state statutes for confirmation as well.

The following information addresses signs of child abuse, elder abuse, spousal abuse, and sexual abuse.

Disclaimer: I am neither a clinician nor a licensed social worker, counselor, or mental healthcare worker qualified to diagnose any of the issues listed below. However, I have encountered these signs through endless 9-1-1 responses throughout my career as a law enforcement professional, and you may have as well, even if you didn't recognize them at the time.

The following provides a general overview of the indicators associated with various forms of abuse, including child abuse, elder abuse, spousal abuse, and sexual abuse. Recognizing these indicators is crucial for timely intervention and support for affected individuals.

Child Abuse

Identifying the signs of child abuse can be complex; however, it is essential to recognize several indicators that a child may be subjected to mistreatment.

Abuse may occur in various forms, including physical, emotional, sexual, or neglectful, and each category may exhibit distinct manifestations. Below are critical signs that warrant attention:

Signs of Physical Abuse:

> Unexplained Injuries: Look for bruises, burns, cuts, or fractures that do not have a clear origin. These injuries can manifest in various stages of healing and may appear in unusual patterns—perhaps in the shape of fingers or on vulnerable soft areas of the body like the face, neck, or back.
>
> Frequent Injuries: A child who frequently sustains injuries—such as broken bones, sprains, or burns, without a reasonable explanation—may be experiencing physical abuse. It's important to consider how often these bumps and bruises occur.
>
> Fear of Physical Contact: The child may exhibit a noticeable flinch or cringe at the slightest touch, showing an instinctual fear, particularly when approached by specific individuals. This can be a significant indicator of past trauma.
>
> Reluctance to Go Home: A child exhibiting anxiety or outright fear about returning home may be trying to communicate discomfort with their living situation. They might express concerns about being with certain family members, which can suggest a troubled environment.
>
> Visible Marks or Scratches: Note any visible marks or scratches on the child's body. These may indicate signs of being roughly handled—such as grip marks on their arms—showing that they have been subjected to physical aggression.

Emotional or Psychological Abuse:

> Low self-esteem or self-harm: A child experiencing emotional abuse may show profound signs of insecurity and self-hatred. This can manifest in distressing behaviors such as cutting or other forms of self-harm, as they struggle to cope with their feelings.

Fear, anxiety, or depression: A child may frequently display intense sadness or chronic anxiety, leading to withdrawal from peers and activities they once enjoyed. They might exhibit fearfulness that seems disproportionate to their surroundings, often without an identifiable cause.

Difficulty forming relationships: Due to underlying anxiety or deep-seated trust issues, the child may shy away from making new friends or forming close connections. They may feel apprehensive in social situations, finding it hard to engage with others or maintain relationships.

Behavioral extremes: Emotional abuse may lead to drastic shifts in behavior. The child might become excessively obedient and compliant, often trying to please others at the expense of their own needs, or conversely, they might act out with aggression or defiance, lashing out at those around them.

Regression in behavior: A child may revert to earlier developmental stages, such as a potty-trained child starting to wet the bed again or reverting to thumb-sucking. They may take on behaviors typically associated with much younger children, indicating a struggle with their emotional state.

Avoidance of certain situations or people: The child may exhibit a strong tendency to avoid specific adults or caregivers, feeling anxious or unsafe in their presence. This avoidance may extend to particular places or situations where they associate fear or distress.

Sexual Abuse:

Difficulty Walking or Sitting: The child may experience physical discomfort in certain areas or show signs of genital injury and other areas of the body near the genital regions.

Sexual Knowledge Beyond Their Age: The child might discuss sexual topics or exhibit sexual behaviors that are not developmentally appropriate.

Unexplained sexually transmitted diseases (STDs) or Genital Infections: Signs of sexually transmitted diseases or injuries to the genitals may suggest sexual abuse.

Fear of a Particular Person: The child may express fear or avoidance of a specific individual, often the perpetrator.

Torn or Stained Clothing: Underwear or other clothing may show signs of being torn or stained inappropriately.

Sexualized Behavior: Engaging in sexual acts or behaviors with other children or adults, especially if deemed inappropriate for their age.

Neglect:

Poor Hygiene or Dirty Clothes: The child may have a consistently dirty appearance, exhibit bad body odor, or have unkempt hair.

Unexplained Weight Loss or Malnutrition: They may appear unusually thin, malnourished, or frequently hungry.

Untreated Medical Conditions: Due to a lack of medical care, neglected children might have untreated injuries, illnesses, or chronic conditions.

Inadequate Supervision: The child may be left alone for extended periods without proper care or supervision for their age.

Lack of Appropriate Clothing for the Weather: The child may wear unsuitable clothing for the season, such as no coat in winter or no hat in summer.

Behavioral Signs of Possible Abuse:

Frequent Absences or Tardiness from School: A child who is often absent or late may be attempting to escape an uncomfortable or unsafe home environment.

This behavior could signal that they are trying to avoid returning home or that circumstances at home are preventing them from attending school altogether.

Aggressive or Disruptive Behavior: Some children who experience abuse may express their emotions through aggression. This can manifest as fighting, acting out in class, or exhibiting violent tendencies towards peers. Such behavior often stems from their inability to process the trauma they are enduring.

Extreme Clinginess or Attachment: When a child exhibits an intense need for closeness to adults or caregivers, it may be a result of fear or insecurity stemming from their home life.

This overly dependent behavior can appear as an excessive need for attention, constant reassurance, or reluctance to leave the side of trusted adults.

Difficulty Concentrating or Learning: Emotional turmoil can severely hinder a child's cognitive abilities. When a child is struggling with feelings of fear, anxiety, or depression due to abuse, they may find it incredibly challenging to focus on schoolwork and participate in learning activities, leading to a decline in academic performance.

Social Withdrawal or Dissociation: A child who feels unsafe may start to distance themselves from their peers. This could manifest as avoidance of playdates, reluctance to join group activities, or complete isolation from other children and adults. They may appear sad, withdrawn, or detached from the world around them.

Signs of Abusive Caregivers or Abusive Family Dynamics:

Overly Harsh or Inconsistent Discipline: Caregivers who employ severe or erratic punishment techniques often contribute to a child's fear and distress. Their reluctance to discuss the child's injuries or behavior may further indicate an unhealthy dynamic.

Blaming the Child: Caregivers who frequently blame the child for household issues or express negative opinions about them in public can damage the child's self-esteem. This constant criticism can create feelings of worthlessness or shame in the child.

Substance Abuse: Caregivers who struggle with addiction may neglect their responsibilities, leading to potential abuse or emotional neglect of the child. Their impairment can create an unstable home environment where the child's needs are overlooked.

Isolating the Child: When caregivers keep a child away from friends, family, or community activities, it can indicate a desire to control the child's environment.

Such isolation can prevent the child from forming healthy relationships and participating in essential social experiences.

Defensive or Evasive Behavior: Caregivers who respond with anger, defensiveness, or secrecy when questioned about the child's welfare may be trying to hide something. Their reactions can signal an awareness of problematic situations and an unwillingness to address them openly.

Elder Abuse

Elder abuse can manifest in various troubling ways, and it is vital to recognize the signs early to prevent further harm and obtain the necessary help. This abuse can take on physical, emotional, financial, or neglectful forms. Below are detailed indicators to be aware of:

Physical Abuse:

Look for unexplained bruises, burns, cuts, or fractures that might suggest violent encounters or mishandling.

Pay attention to injuries that appear to be in different stages of healing. This indicates a pattern of ongoing harm.

Observing significant weight loss or signs of malnutrition can signal that the elder is not receiving adequate nourishment.

Poor personal hygiene or unsanitary living conditions could point to neglect, suggesting that their basic needs are not being met.

Notice any withdrawal from social activities or an elder's reluctance to talk about their injuries, which may indicate fear or shame.

Emotional or Psychological Abuse:

Sudden and dramatic mood swings, anxiety, or signs of depression may indicate emotional distress caused by mistreatment.

If the elder is increasingly withdrawn from family and friends or avoids social interactions, it could be a sign of psychological abuse.

An inexplicable fear of certain people or a refusal to speak when they are present may show that the elder feels threatened or unsafe.

Low self-esteem and helplessness can manifest when individuals are consistently manipulated or belittled by caregivers.

Look for signs that the elder becomes submissive or fearful in the presence of a caregiver, indicating a toxic dynamic.

Financial Abuse:

Financial abuse is not discussed very often. Older adults may not report financial abuse for several reasons, many of which are tied to fear, shame, manipulation, or a lack of awareness.

Be alert to unexplained or suspicious withdrawals of money or sudden large financial transactions that don't align with prior behavior.

Unusual activity in bank accounts or missing valuables might suggest someone is inappropriately handling the elderly's finances.

If the elder signs documents—like a will or power of attorney—without fully understanding their implications, this could indicate exploitation.

The elder may express feelings of coercion or pressure to give away money or assets to someone else, signaling financial manipulation.

Neglect:

Unattended medical conditions, injuries, or skin problems should raise concerns about the level of care being provided.

Indicators of poor personal hygiene, dirty clothing, or improper attire for the weather reflect neglect of basic personal care.

Unexpected weight loss or signs of dehydration are serious red flags that indicate insufficient nourishment or hydration.

Lack of access to food, basic necessities, or proper medical care can highlight a dangerous neglect of the elderly's fundamental needs.

Unsafe living conditions, such as inadequate heating, lack of running water, or poor lighting, can create hazardous environments for the elderly.

Adult Sexual Abuse

The sensitive subject of adult sexual abuse frequently compels individuals to turn a blind eye or dismiss the possibility that such incidents occur within their church or small town. However, the stark reality is that sexual abuse impacts a far greater number of individuals than one might assume.

Much like the subtle traits of financial abuse, a significant number of victims choose not to report instances of sexual abuse due to an overwhelming fear of retaliation or a deep sense of embarrassment.

Understanding the warning signs associated with sexual abuse can allow observers to offer crucial support to those who may be suffering in silence. Recognizing these signs is essential in creating a safe environment where victims feel encouraged to seek professional help and behavioral/clinical counseling.

> Unexplained bruising in the genital area or the presence of sexually transmitted infections requires immediate concern and investigation, as well as behavioral and clinical intervention.

> Difficulty walking or sitting, along with other unexplained physical discomforts, can indicate inappropriate physical interactions.

> A reluctance to be touched or a palpable fear of certain individuals could signal a history of inappropriate advances or touches.

Spousal Abuse
Spousal abuse, often referred to as domestic violence, encompasses a range of abusive behaviors that can be classified into several categories: physical, emotional, psychological, sexual, and financial abuse. Each form can leave deep and lasting scars on the victim, affecting not only their physical well-being but also their mental and emotional health, and yes, even death.

Identifying the signs of spousal abuse can be particularly difficult, as victims frequently grapple with feelings of shame, fear, or manipulation that compel them to keep the abuse hidden from others. They might feel trapped in their situation, leading to isolation from friends and family who could offer support.

Here are some key indicators to be aware of when assessing the presence of spousal abuse:

Signs of Physical Abuse

> Unexplained Injuries: One of the most telling signs of physical abuse is when an individual has bruises, cuts, burns, or fractures that they cannot adequately explain. Often, these injuries are accompanied by inconsistent or vague explanations. Look for injuries that might be deliberately concealed in sensitive areas like the neck, face, or arms.
>
> Frequent Doctor Visits: A victim of physical abuse may find themselves visiting the doctor or emergency room more often than normal.
>
> These medical visits are typically due to injuries that require attention, yet they often lack a clear or credible explanation for their condition, raising concerns about the underlying cause.
>
> Fear of Being Touched: A notable indicator of abuse is a victim's reaction to touch. If they flinch or visibly tense up when approached or touched by their partner, this can signal a deep-seated fear rooted in past experiences of violence or aggression.
>
> Recurring "Accidents: Abusers may refer to injuries as having occurred during "accidents." However, a pattern of such "accidents" can emerge, suggesting that these incidents may actually be a thinly veiled cover for ongoing physical abuse.
>
> Bruises and Injuries in Various Stages of Healing: When a victim displays bruises or injuries that are at different stages of healing, it can be a strong indicator of repetitive abuse. This pattern points to a cycle of violence that is often hidden from view, making it crucial to recognize these signs for what they truly represent.

Emotional or Psychological Abuse:

> Relentless Criticism: The abuser systematically belittles and insults their partner, deeply eroding their self-worth and sense of identity. This could also be listed as verbal abuse.
>
> Manipulative Gaslighting: Victims are made to question their sanity as the abuser distorts the truth and denies abusive actions, leaving them confused and isolated.
>
> Fear through Intimidation: The abuser instills fear by threatening violence or harm, creating a toxic environment where control is paramount.
>
> Isolation Tactics: Victims are often disconnected from their support networks, as the abuser monitors interactions and discourages contact with friends and family.
>
> Induced Guilt: Victims come to believe they bear responsibility for the abuse, wrongly thinking they provoke the abuser's behavior.
>
> Possessiveness and Jealousy: The abuser's excessive jealousy breeds insecurity and anxiety in the victim, reinforcing their feeling of entrapment and fear.

Financial Abuse:

> Control over finances: The abuser often exerts a significant degree of control over the victim's financial resources, effectively eliminating their independence. This control can manifest in various ways, such as denying the victim access to joint or individual bank accounts, limiting their ability to withdraw cash, or requiring permission to spend money.
>
> The victim may find themselves in a position where they must demonstrate need or justify their purchases, leading to a dynamic of dependency.

As this situation unfolds, the victim's financial autonomy diminishes, making them reliant on the abuser for even the most basic financial decisions.

Withholding money or resources: The abuser may resort to withholding not only money but also essential resources necessary for the victim's day-to-day survival.

This may include restricting access to funds needed for groceries, appropriate clothing, transportation, and healthcare.

The abuser may strategically prevent the victim from accessing money for necessary medical care or prescriptions, leading to health deterioration over time.

This form of abuse reinforces a power imbalance, keeping the victim in a continuous state of vulnerability and uncertainty regarding their basic needs.

Preventing employment: The abuser frequently undermines the victim's professional aspirations and employment opportunities. This can include active sabotage, such as damaging the victim's reputation with potential employers, restricting their ability to attend job interviews, or even creating situations that force the victim to leave their job. The abuser may also exert control over the victim's schedule, making it impossible for them to pursue job training or development opportunities. This constant interference not only affects the victim's ability to earn an income but also erodes their self-esteem and sense of capability, reinforcing their dependency on the abuser.

Forced financial decisions: The abuser often pressures the victim into making financial decisions that only serve the abuser's interests. Such coercion can include forcing the victim to sign contracts, take out loans, or incur debts without a clear understanding of the consequences.

The victim might be led to believe that these decisions are necessary for their mutual benefit, even though they primarily enrich the abuser or entrap the victim in a cycle of debt.

Over time, these forced decisions can lead to serious financial repercussions, affecting the victim's credit score and financial stability, while simultaneously tightening the abuser's grip on the victim's life.

Control and Manipulation:

Monitoring Communications: The abuser often keeps a watchful eye on the victim's communications, invading their privacy by monitoring phone calls, emails, text messages, and social media activities. This invasive behavior is designed to isolate the victim from friends, family, and support networks, making it difficult for them to seek help or maintain their independence.

Constant Surveillance: The victim may feel as if they are under constant scrutiny, as the abuser tracks their movements or follows them closely. The abuser frequently demands detailed reports on the victim's whereabouts, creating an atmosphere of fear and anxiety where the victim feels they cannot go anywhere without permission or oversight.

Extreme Controlling Behavior: The abuser exerts overwhelming control over the victim's daily life. This can include dictating what the victim should wear, where they are allowed to go, who they can spend time with, and how they should allocate their free time. Such controlling behavior strips the victim of their autonomy and self-expression, leaving them feeling powerless and trapped.

Threats to Harm Loved Ones or Pets: To manipulate and instill fear in the victim, the abuser may issue chilling threats to harm the victim's children, family members, or pets. This tactic is intended to create an emotional response, forcing the victim to comply with the abuser's demands out of fear for the safety of their loved ones. This cruel strategy reinforces the abuser's power and control over the victim's life.

Behavioral Signs in an Abused Spouse:

Withdrawal or Isolation: The victim often retreats into themselves, becoming increasingly disengaged from friends and family.

They may decline invitations to social events, preferring solitude over the anxiety of interacting with others, which stems from feelings of fear or shame about their situation.

Fear of Their Partner: When the abuser is nearby, the victim might display noticeable signs of distress, such as flinching at sudden movements or avoiding direct eye contact.

This constant state of anxiety compels them to tread carefully to prevent conflict, reflecting an overwhelming desire to keep the abuser calm and avoid any potential outbursts.

Self-Blame: It is common for the victim to internalize the abuse, often expressing remorse for the abuser's behavior. They may vocally justify the mistreatment, firmly believing that they deserve it or that their actions can somehow prevent further incidents, creating a cycle of guilt and responsibility placed unfairly upon themselves.

Changes in Behavior or Personality: The effects of abuse can profoundly alter the victim's demeanor. They may become increasingly anxious, withdrawn, or even exhibit signs of depression. This shift in personality often manifests as a loss of confidence and a pervasive sense of hopelessness, indicative of their ongoing struggle against the abuse.

Physical Symptoms of Stress: The toll of the abusive situation can lead to a variety of chronic stress symptoms.

The victim might suffer from insomnia, persistent anxiety, significant weight fluctuations, and a host of unexplained physical ailments. These symptoms are not just emotional but manifest physically, reflecting the intense pressure they endure.

Frequent Absences from Work or Social Gatherings: The victim may find themselves frequently missing work or social commitments. Often, this avoidance is driven by fear of the abuser's reaction if they leave home, or it may serve as a means to conceal injuries that they are trying to hide. Their absences become a coping mechanism rooted in vulnerability and fear, further isolating them from support networks.

Signs of an Abuser

Overly Controlling Behavior: An abuser often exhibits a need for control that can manifest in various ways. They may insist that the victim carries out tasks exactly as they dictate, and they might issue threats to impose consequences if their demands are not met. This behavior creates a power imbalance, leaving the victim feeling helpless and coerced.

History of Aggression or Violence: Many abusers have a documented history of violent actions or severe emotional outbursts. This can include episodes of rage that are directed not only at the victim but also towards others, showcasing a pattern of aggression that instills fear and anxiety in those around them.

Blaming the Victim: A common tactic used by abusers is to deflect blame onto the victim. They may assert that the victim's actions or attitudes "provoked" the abuse, fostering a false narrative where the victim is made to feel responsible for the abuser's violent behavior. This manipulative strategy confuses the victim, leaving them questioning their own perceptions of reality.

Inconsistent Apologies or "Honeymoon Phase": Following an incident of abuse, an abuser may shift dramatically in behavior, becoming overly apologetic or affectionate. This "honeymoon phase" can make the victim feel momentarily safe and loved, but it is often short-lived. The abuser eventually reverts to their abusive tendencies, returning to a cycle of manipulation that keeps the victim emotionally trapped.

As I mentioned earlier, I am neither a clinician, a behaviorist, nor a licensed medical professional. The above information was not meant for church security to diagnose all situations. It was designed to provide information on 'potential' warning signs. The information is not exhaustive, as there is so much information on each particular topic and subtopic. Hopefully, however, the information will make you look at things differently, now that you know some of the signs. In law enforcement, we operate under the rule of 'The totality of the circumstances.'

What this means is police must consider all relevant facts, factors, and conditions in any given situation, rather than just focusing on a single piece of evidence or fact. A man running down the street at 3:00 a.m. does not make him a criminal. A child with a fresh scratch on the forehead does not necessarily mean child abuse. Your security team and your workers must look at numerous *'signs'* or behaviors prior to accusing anyone of abuse. I encourage the leadership team, your elders, your security team, and your volunteers to participate in the training listed earlier. It will only help.

My last thought about why knowing what the signs are and how/when to report those signs is this: When congregation members show signs of abuse, a well-trained security team can recognize the warning signs, respond with discretion and compassion, and take appropriate steps to ensure the individual's safety while following church policies and legal requirements.

Chapter Nine
FACILITIES

If your church is located in a small strip mall or rents a storefront, you probably have one or two doors at the front and a wall full of windows. While these windows can be a great way to let natural light in, they can also present a challenge when it comes to signage and advertising. The first step to take is to review your lease agreement with the property management company to see if and how much signage they allow.

When thinking about how to use your windows to promote your church or current season, it's important to consider aesthetics. Too much information plastered on the windows can look messy and overwhelming, and may give the impression of desperation or unprofessionalism. Additionally, it can block visibility in the parking lot, making it difficult for people to see when they're trying to find your church. In the event of an emergency or critical incident, it can also hinder first responders' view inside.

If you have a nursery room near the front of your church, it's a good idea to install some film or covering on the windows to prevent people from looking inside. This will help create a more private and secure environment for the children and their families.

Storefront churches are usually small in size and have one or two entrance doors and the same number of rear doors. While the primary function of the rear doors is for emergency exits, they are also used for taking out the trash.

When setting up security protocols, it is crucial to consider the security of the rear doors. The rear doors area should not be used for storage or blocked in any way to ensure easy access in case of emergency. This area should always be kept clear to allow for easy ingress and egress.

A good locking mechanism for the rear doors should be used, which does not interfere with emergency exiting. These doors should be locked during service times, and after the service, they should be checked to ensure they are still locked when everyone leaves for the day. It is also a good idea to install cameras both outside and inside the rear doors, as it is essential to know who is coming and going.

Access to facilities
This book has discussed, in detail, the protocols for dealing with entry while in service, but have you thought about those days when no services are scheduled, yet the building is still being used? Safety does not stop just because the congregation is absent or no little kids are running around. Having protocols in place helps maintain security and safeguard property and prevents the 'spur of the moment crime of opportunity'. And it does not matter if you are leading a large or small church; safety is safety. However, if you rent space from a school or another church, your options may be limited to the rules and regulations of those facilities.

Limiting access and clearly defining who is authorized to enter the facility is not only recommended, but it needs to be enforced. If you have church staff, volunteers, and handymen helping, they each need to understand when they can be in the building and when it is time to leave. You can specify certain hours for each. Normal business hours will suffice for most days. If you are planning a large event, such as a Christmas activity or a Harvest festival, then optional considerations need to be addressed.

For vendors and visitors, having a check-in procedure, including requiring IDs or issuing temporary badges, should be considered. Using a sign-in sheet (paper or digital) will help identify and track those who visited the church. Requiring them to produce a picture ID is sound practice. Asking for an ID will also help in identifying those who may have caused past problems or who have been trespassed previously. Listing the reason they are in the facility will assist you in determining future operational needs. You will be able to identify the patterns of deliveries, when volunteers usually show up, and so on.

When people visit, and they will be there for some time, provide a visitor badge. This badge should be numbered and a completely different color from those of the staff or volunteers. It should also indicate if limited access is granted to certain areas of the church facilities. For vendors, there is no need to issue visitor badges. They usually drop off, and then they leave. However, if they are required to take a package(s) elsewhere, it may be quicker just to have a volunteer or staff member escort them. Your escort policy should clearly outline who will escort visitors, the date, and the reason they were on site.

If keys are issued to designated people, there needs to be a key log maintained and updated as needed. It seems everyone wants a key to the church. You must sound judgments on whom to issue keys to. Not everyone needs a key. The more keys roaming around, the more problems there will be. Those with keys must be held to a very high standard when it comes to either opening up the facilities at the proper time or securing them at the proper time. Those with access during the off days must understand the importance of locking up when leaving.

Remember, your church and associated facilities are considered private property, and you have the right to determine what check-in procedures work best for the church.

Every church is different with unique needs. Take a very hard look at those requesting keys. Ask yourself:
1. Why do they want a key?
2. Do I need them to have a key?

If you cannot answer both in a positive, definite response, they likely do not need a key.

Understanding the specific needs of your facilities will help you develop protocols for visitors and key distributions. In the end, not everyone will be happy. Some may not want to show their IDs. Yet, they are asking permission to enter a private property setting. You and your staff decide the rules. Others might be upset that they did not have a key issued to them. If they become upset over that, then you made the right decision by not giving them a key.

Sharing a building

There are times when different churches must combine their resources and share a facility. Through the *Protection With Grace, LLC* survey, data suggests the percentage of churches renting to other churches could be as high as 18%. The renting of one to another is not a bad thing and should never be viewed as such. My church rents to another, and both co-exist fine. This section does not deal with a church renting from a school. As mentioned, different aspects of protocols and laws are brought in. This section only deals with one church renting from another.

Sharing a building can be rewarding, cost-effective, and a great way to bridge the gap and build relationships with other congregations. However, it can also come with challenges. Hopefully, the following will help guide you through the process if you decide to rent to others or need to rent from an established church.

Communication is a must. I am not just talking about the schedule. There needs to be open and honest communication regarding the needs, the maintenance, and shared concerns. By bringing in another church, they have access to everything in the common areas. Sharing of phone numbers and contact information for key employees will help in the communication process, especially during emergencies.

Creating a shared calendar will help with the scheduling of events and could even lead to participating in events together, to help build those relationships. This creates a record of who was present when an issue occurred.

Don't let small issues become bigger issues. Communication is the key. If problems are brewing, address them immediately. You likely have a shared faith, so always start with the Word to help guide you through problems. Most conflicts arise out of misunderstandings or perceived wrongdoings. Through regularly scheduled meetings, most issues can be handled immediately, which in turn allows instant communication back to the respective leaders. Do not let small issues become big issues.

There needs to be a written agreement between both parties. This should not be overlooked or reduced to a "We don't need a lawyer; we can do it ourselves" mentality. Draft a formal agreement, detailing schedules, maintenance, and financial obligations. Add in a process for resolving any conflicts or disagreements. Having a decision-making matrix in place will let everyone know exactly what steps to take in case there are misunderstandings. This formality should not be considered out of line. As a matter of fact, it should be welcomed by both entities as each is protected.

Any signed agreement should include the shared responsibilities. This means there is a open understanding of open and locking procedures.

There are clearly defined responsibilities for keeping the common areas secure and clean. Thoughtful consideration should be given to the use of any shared equipment. It has been my experience that this usually pertains to the electronics, instruments for the Praise and Worship, and other aspects of the service. However, it could also include kitchen supplies. A signed agreement allows for expectations to be read, discussed, and understood.

Depending on the size of your facility or the one you wish to rent from, you may have common areas, and you may have inaccessible areas. Respect those areas. Your agreement should indicate those areas.

The recommendation to not share office space is preferred. These are the areas that contain most of the sensitive data (operational and congregational information) and should not be shared. I also recommend not sharing the computers or electronic files. These need to be kept separate.

As discussed earlier about the issuing of keys, it becomes paramount to know who has the keys and the alarm code. Those who are renting to another need to know exactly who has the keys. Usually, churches that rent from another are smaller, so the number of keys issued is lower anyway.

Through your agreement, you will need to itemize, label, and project possible expenses. Based on the number of days and people attending from the new church, cleaning expenses and utility expenses (heat, air conditioning, water, electricity) will all increase. Be open, from the beginning, about the financial requirements. If you are renting to another, you are not obligated to disclose all your financials to them, nor are they obligated to do the same. Yet, through a written agreement, there should be no misunderstandings about monthly expenses, what they are for, and when payments are due. Remember, this is not a bad thing; it is just business.

Security from each church should meet and discuss protocols, suggestion rally points, phone numbers, and email exchanges. They also need to meet to review mandated safety policies established by the main church.

Understanding that not every church operates exactly the same will help you decide who you want to rent from or to. There will always be differences. If you know what those are, you can communicate with the other to eliminate any confusion about what is taking place in the church facilities. Nowhere in your agreement should you be mandated to perform or not perform any function that goes against your faith.

The sharing of facilities is more about expanding the Word of God than about one church renting from another. By allowing a smaller church to use your facility, you are providing a safe place for people to worship. If you are a new church and you rent, you are on the front line of learning protocols and practices you may want to incorporate into your facility someday.

Cameras and installation topics

I strongly believe that visible cameras are better than hidden cameras. I have cameras installed on my house and intentionally made them visible to anyone who walks by or up to my house. Ideally, cameras should be visible and must be seen by everyone. The most important reason for a camera is safety and protection. Based on statistical studies, a visible camera has a good probability of reducing suspicious activities that can lead to break-ins and vandalism. A camera is a deterrent to any potential break-in or intruder, and it reduces the probability of a risk for a potential crime as a function of "We are Watching." As a former law enforcement officer, I know criminals tend to target places with no cameras or lights. So, why install cameras that people cannot see? I suggest installing visible cameras and lights to let the world know that your property is being monitored.

To ensure a transparent and trustworthy relationship with your congregation, it is advisable to communicate clearly with them about the installation of surveillance cameras. You should provide them with a detailed explanation about the reasons for their installation and how they will be used. This will help to assure your employees and members of the congregation that the cameras are being used for their safety and protection.

You may want to consider certain areas when purchasing and installing cameras. Where should the outside cameras be installed? What about the inside cameras? Should I buy Wi-Fi cameras or wired cameras? The list of questions is endless, but let's stick with these three.

Regarding the outside camera installation question, there are some things to consider:

1. Entrance and exit doors will always be a must. You need to know who is coming and going. Someone vetted by the church leadership should be appointed to review the videos once a week.
2. Being able to view the parking lot is essential. Vehicles are susceptible to theft and vandalism, especially during the evening hours.
3. Cameras installed in a manner to view the perimeter of your property should be considered. This can help monitor any unauthorized access and can help determine how people arrived and in what direction they left.
4. If your church has an outside playground or gathering place for events, please install cameras to monitor these areas.
5. It is highly recommended that printed signs with a disclaimer such as "Security cameras are recording all activities 24/7" be visible. The more cameras and signs that provide information that cameras are continually

video recording all activities will likely reduce the probability of any unforeseen event resulting in vandalism or criminal activity. A video camera is akin to having ferocious dogs protecting the perimeter of a given area.

One must understand the laws of your local area when installing outdoor cameras that might record other people. Generally, it is legal to record in public places, but it could become an issue if your cameras capture footage inside someone else's home or on their property. It is essential to be aware of the camera's field of view, as people have a legitimate expectation of privacy. The best way to ensure the church is not infringing on anyone's right to privacy is to seek legal advice, obtain such legal advice in writing, and distribute it to all congregants. Transparency is the key to being inclusive while avoiding legal disputes.

When discussing inside cameras, churches need to exercise discretion and sensitivity to respect the privacy and sanctity of the space. You must consider specific areas within the church where cameras should typically not be placed.

This is to ensure that the installation of cameras does not infringe upon the privacy of the congregants or detract from the sanctity of the space.

All 50 states have laws in place that provide privileged communication between clergy. Cameras should not be installed where counseling or private conversations occur.

These spaces are considered sacred, and privacy is a must. Placing cameras in areas where any part of the restrooms and/or changing rooms can be viewed violates people's privacy and can have legal consequences due to privacy laws.

Suppose your church has any 'sacred' places where religious ceremonies or rituals are performed. In that case, you might consider whether camera installation would interfere with or disrespect the ritual. Any counseling rooms should also be deemed confidential. Installing a camera in these types of rooms seriously hampers any type of trust you are building with your employees or members.

Some say cameras should not be installed in such a manner as to capture a person being baptized. That is your decision. I have seen churches record the event and provide a copy to the baptized person, and I have seen live streams from churches of baptized people. Again, based on your beliefs, cameras set up to capture these events are best left up to you and the church.

The decision to use wi-fi cameras or those that are hardwired into a system is based on your facilities (own, rent, size, limitations) and your budget. Wi-Fi cameras are easy to install since no cables run through walls or ceilings. They work great if you know you only rent for a short time.

Since they can be placed almost anywhere, you have more flexibility for positioning, and if you decide to change the layout of a room or hallway, you can move them quickly.

These cameras can usually be accessed remotely. It is ideal to allow a few trusted members access to the camera system since, at any given time, someone might be on vacation or busy with life issues.

Wi-Fi cameras are susceptible to hacking and interference from nearby electronic devices or networks. If your church is located in a small strip mall, then interference could be an issue. Additionally, these cameras require a power source.

Cameras are available that are powered by rechargeable batteries or ones that can be plugged into an outlet. Depending on the layout of your facilities, one or more of these options is desirable. If batteries are needed or recharged, adding an inspection schedule for the cameras might be feasible.

In the realm of surveillance cameras, hardwired cameras are typically considered more reliable than their Wi-Fi counterparts. This is due to their ability to transmit data through cables, reducing susceptibility to hacking and interference from nearby devices or networks.

Hardwired cameras can still be monitored and controlled remotely despite their reliance on cables. Furthermore, such camera systems often come equipped with a recording device, which should be kept in a secure location accessible only to a select few individuals. It is important to note that the placement of the recording device is a crucial aspect of the security system, and should be carefully considered to ensure maximum protection.

The cost of setting up a hardwired camera system is usually higher than that of a Wi-Fi system. Unless someone within the church is knowledgeable and capable of installing the system, it is advisable to hire a professional installer.

Additionally, relocating cameras to other areas within the church or to a different location can be expensive. To my knowledge, churches that rent space do not typically have a hardwired system in place.

Either system will allow for recording to be activated, and most come with some type of audible alarm or the ability to let the intruder know you are watching (two-way talk mode).

To ensure that your Wi-Fi or hardwired camera system is working efficiently, it's important to establish protocols for regular inspections.

This will help you keep track of whether monitoring and recording are up-to-date and operational. It's recommended that you allow more than one person to have access to viewing and settings for the camera systems, including passwords. It is highly recommended that passwords be changed once per month and that passwords be secured. Security passwords should have alphanumeric characters and other additional marks such as $, #, &, @. If any of your staff or volunteers leave, you must change the password access immediately to maintain security.

Electric control panels
Electrical control panels should be secured with a lock. You want to ensure safety, maintain security systems, and protect the operational integrity of your electrical system. As mentioned earlier, with smaller churches, a few people may have many roles. And at times, some of those roles can become mixed. Only those with knowledge of the facility and the panels should have access. When you lock the panel(s), you are not only thinking of safety first (preventing access to dangerous electrical equipment and components), but you are accomplishing the following:

1. You are preventing tampering attempts against intentional or unintentional, unauthorized access. With locks in place, you are ensuring only those who should have access do.
2. In reality, it could be the law in your area. You may have regulatory laws or codes to adhere to. Honestly, even if there is no such compliance mandate, it still bodes well to go above and beyond the safety requirements for your facility.
3. The risk of accidental or unauthorized modifications to the settings is a real concern. Such

changes can lead to serious consequences, such as equipment malfunction or process disruptions.
4. Protecting data is another important aspect of this topic. Locked panels could prevent the loss of sensitive information and operational data. Having locked panels provides an essential layer of security.

Access to these panels needs to be restricted to those who either have experience or know-how (facility manager) or have been assigned an operational responsibility in case of emergencies (Security). If none of the above arguments work, I will add this last point. Keeping little hands out of any electrical panel should be the most important reason for installing locks. Kids will be kids, and sometimes, they do not know what they are playing with. Conversations should be had with the children attending your church. But we know conversations only last so long. Put the locks on the panels.

Storage of hazardous materials

According to the Federal Emergency Management Administration (FEMA), storage of hazardous supplies can be defined as:

> *Substances or materials, which, because of their chemical, physical, or biological nature, pose a potential risk to life, health, or property if they are released.*
>
> *A "release" may occur by spilling, leaking, emitting toxic vapors, or any other process that enables the material to escape its container, enter the environment, and create a potential hazard. Hazards are classified in many different ways. The following introduces several common terms:*

1. *Explosive substances release pressure, gas, and heat suddenly when they are subjected to shock, heat, or high pressure. Fourth of July celebrations use many types of explosive substances that require careful storage and handling to avoid injury.*

2. *Flammable and combustible substances are easy to ignite. Paint thinners, charcoal lighter fluid, and silver polish are all highly flammable. Oxidizers, which will lend oxygen readily to support a fire, and reactive materials, which are unstable and may react violently if mishandled, pose related hazards.*

3. *Poisons (or toxic materials) can cause injury or death when they enter the bodies of living things. Such substances can be classified by chemical nature (for example, heavy metals and cyanides) or by toxic action (such as irritants, which inflame living tissue, and corrosives, which destroy or irreversibly change it). One special group of poisons includes etiological (biological) agents. These are live microorganisms, or toxins produced by these microorganisms, that are capable of producing a disease.*

4. *Radioactive materials are a category of hazardous materials that release harmful radiation. They are not addressed specifically in this course.*

These categories are not mutually exclusive. For example, acids and bases are listed as corrosive materials, but can also act as poisons.

Definition of Hazardous Materials.

Emergency Management Institute redirects page. (n.d.). https://emilms.fema.gov/is_0005a/groups/134.html

With the above information, it is safe to assume that storing hazardous materials in closed closets can pose a significant risk to everyone in the building. Combining materials, such as cleaning supplies/chemicals, paint, sanitizers, and insect extermination chemicals, can easily lead to accidental spills, leaks, fires, or harmful fumes.

Hazardous materials should be stored in areas that are designed to handle such items. Interior wall closets are not designed to have proper ventilation to the outside, yet that is where the materials are stored. The areas need proper ventilation and doors that can be locked so little ones cannot access the material. Without ventilation, harmful fumes or vapors can accumulate quickly. I have seen where cleaning supplies and paint were stored in the electrical closets or the closet/space for the water heater. Both are bad ideas since most hazardous fumes are flammable.

If material is stored on the property, please keep all the labels on the containers. This will help identify potential dangers and precautions for handling. Instead of using interior closets, consider using a shelving system designed to hold the materials or rooms with exterior walls. Both will provide some type of ventilation to alleviate the buildup of harmful fumes or vapors.

If your church is small like mine and there are limited spaces to store such material, please consult with your local fire department or professionals in the environmental health and safety field to determine best practices. They will be able to tell what chemicals are compatible and which ones may have a negative or hazardous reaction with each other, as well as provide some direction on how to store materials properly.

The following is from Sergeant Tom Page, who worked for the Las Vegas Metropolitan Police Department for 25 years and retired as a Special Events Sergeant.

He has 6 years of experience as Director of Security for the UFC, 8 years as the Law Enforcement Coordinator for the Veterans Tribute CTA High School, and prior Director of Security for the Neon Museum. He does private protection details as well as instructs at numerous churches in both Active Shooter and Conflict Management scenarios.

When I think about church security, I think of Ephesians 6:11, "Put on the whole armor of God, that you may be able to stand against the wiles of the Devil."

As with the selection of personnel and training, the armor of God is part of the preparation, as stated against the wiles of the Devil. This means that churches need to first believe that the wiles of the Devil, in whatever form, will come to their door, will not be. A soldier puts on his armor to prepare for a battle he believes is coming, even before he gets close to and involved in the battle. Churches must do the same and prepare before the battles get close and they are involved.

Why do we have car insurance? We want to be prepared in case we get into an accident. Whose fault the accident is does not matter because you have prepared for the incident with insurance. Have it, and I hope you never need it. A church security ministry/team is the same. Have it and hope they are never needed.

Prepare your church environmentally, with locks, safety tint on windows, cameras, and single points of entry. Do not allow good-hearted members to unlock and open a door that has been secured when they hear a knock. As for personnel, I suggest current or prior security, law enforcement, and military personnel, not for their tactical skills but for their conflict management and verbal Judo skills.

The full armor of God at its foundation is being prepared before an incident.

Tom Page
Sergeant, Retired
Las Vegas Metropolitan Police Department

Unattended bags or boxes left in the church

Churches, like any other business, are susceptible to unknown packages. Identifying a suspicious package can be challenging, as it depends on various factors, and there is no one-size-fits-all description. Reducing the risk of suspicious packages in a church setting involves implementing proactive measures and promoting a vigilant atmosphere. These practices are meant to keep people safe, not to scare them.

It has been my experience that it is usually the residentially challenged who keep and travel with large bags, duffel bags, shopping carts, or backpacks, and those are usually stuffed to the absolute maximum. Remember, this is probably all they own, and they will protect the contents. They are hesitant to leave their possessions unattended as they were, more than likely, a victim of theft before. Yet, allowing such large items in would not be prudent, especially near the food counter. The recommendation is to have a conversation with these owners, and if you can secure the bags, then do so. If not, the only other option is to leave them in a designated area. A recommendation would be to incorporate some type of label system for these large items so your security team can release the items belonging to someone currently visiting or worshipping at the church.

The truly unattended large bags or boxes, in which no one knows the owner, can be a huge security concern if left in or near a church. If this happens, your security team should know and understand the following principles:

>1) Announce to see if anyone will claim the items.
>
>2) If the bag or box truly seems out of place and no one comes forward to claim it, do not touch it, do not move it, or attempt to open it. Notify other security members (if you have more than one) to help keep people out of the area.

3) If you believe the bag(s) dangerous, then evacuate the immediate area and call 9-1-1.

4) When the authorities arrive, tell them where the problem items are and do as directed.

Unattended bags are usually just that—unattended bags, and they may simply belong to someone who is either off visiting in another area of the church or may have accidentally left the items there. Yet, if security justly believes it is a suspicious package, err on the side of caution and take the necessary steps to keep your Congregation safe.

The U.S. Department of Homeland Security provides examples of what a suspicious package may look or feel like. This can be found at www.hsema.dc.gov, or if you would like a digital copy of this book, click on *Characteristics of a Suspicious Package -* https://hsema.dc.gov/sites/default/files/dc/site/hsema/release_content/attachment/20982/Susp_Mail_DHS.PDF

The Homeland Security brochure lists the following:

1. Rigid or bulky
2. Lopsided or uneven
3. Wrapped in a string
4. Badly written or misspelled words
5. Generic or incorrect titles
6. Excessive postage
7. No postage
8. Foreign writing postage, or return address
9. Missing, nonsensical, or unknown return address
10. Leaks, stains, powders, or protruding materials.
11. Ticking, vibration, or other sound

Other characteristics may include:

12. Unusual odors

13. Excessive sealing or taping
14. Unusual shapes or sizes
15. Unusual weight or density

It's important to note that these characteristics are not definitive indicators of a threat, and innocent packages may sometimes exhibit some of these features.

To lessen the risk of a suspicious package being on the property, Security should implement the following:

1. Ensure security constantly walks through and inspects common areas, parking lots, and the perimeter during services or events.
2. Train security members, staff, and volunteers to recognize what may be a suspicious package based on the above descriptors.
3. Train security members, staff, and volunteers on the importance of reporting any concerns.
    a. If the church is in service or there is a church event, security should be notified first.
    b. If there is no service or security on site, 9-1-1 should be called if the package is believed to be suspicious.

Churches/Security retains the right to deny permission for any package or personal property to enter the church. The building itself is private property. Some may claim they cannot leave their possessions outside for fear that they might be stolen. While this may be true, the safety of the congregants is more important. If the Security Supervisor denies entry and the person refuses to leave, it will be treated as a disturbance.

Medical kits in churches

Let's be honest. Most churches, businesses, homes, and cars have a basic first aid kit that includes bandages, out-of-date topical creams, and medications. 95% of the survey respondents stated they had first aid kits on the premises. First aid kits usually have items listed as 'TREAT'. These items can consist of aspirins, antacid tablets, electrolyte tablets, wipes, eye wash, ointments, and creams. These are all perishable.

Having the right first-aid kit(s) on-premise is not the area where you want to buy the cheapest one. Spend a bit of money on a kit that will address more than just the minor boo-boo. Think about what type of injuries or mishaps you will encounter. Don't overthink the contents of the first-aid kit, as most of them are the same.

The location of the first-aid kit is just as essential as having one in the first place. There is no sense in buying a first-aid kit if no one can find it during an emergency. Find a place that is near where the people will be and let everyone know where it is. Communicating this to your congregants should not instill fear, but rather best practices. Depending on the size of your church and the number of buildings, you will need to assess your needs for additional kits. A luncheon, followed by a question-and-answer session with the local Fire Department, will go a long way in both creating relationships and determining what type of first-aid kit you need and where to place them.

Training is crucial for proper first aid, whether it be for a small cut or something more serious. Security should sit down and go through the contents of the first-aid kit to become familiar with the packages and what they are used for.

There is nothing more frustrating than trying to find the right package or ointments during an emergency.

Pre-planning and training before an emergency will help with the outcome of the emergency. There is no harm in asking the Doctors, Nurses, or EMTs in your congregation if they would like to assist with the training. Please remember, however, if they say no, then the answer is no. They might be under contract from their employment, which prohibits private training.

Have you ever thought about the maintenance of the first-aid kit(s)? Most people do not. And it never becomes an issue until an emergency does happen, and needed supplies are not where they are supposed to be. Why does this happen? Everyday life happens, that's why. People get hurt and will reach for a Band-Aid. They will use a compression wrap for an injury that does not require a wrap. They will take out aspirin or eye drops and never replace those items or tell anyone they used them.

And things just seem to disappear. A solution to ensure you have a proper first-aid kit in place is to periodically check it to determine what needs to be replaced based on usage, loss, or expiration dates. Put it on the schedule to check as you would fire extinguishers, locks, and any other items you have on your checklist.

The best first aid kit would include band-aids, topical creams, ice packs, eye rinse, over-the-counter medications, gauze, and trauma wound supplies as well. These are for the most serious injuries. If you do not have anyone at your church with the experience to train others, please reach out to your local fire department or emergency management office for training. Local fire departments, Red Cross and other entities will assist.

Some companies will offer to come in every month and replace your used or missing supplies and this could be a good thing, especially for the larger churches. However, there is a cost to this, and smaller churches will not normally be able to absorb this into their budget. This means the church security team should assigned the responsibility for periodically checking the kits.

There will always be a need for band-aids for minor cuts and scrapes. But have you considered the need for a tourniquet? When people think of the need for tourniquets, they think about gunshot wounds or stabbings near an artery. But in everyday life, tourniquets are used for compound fractures, car accidents, industrial accidents, etc. Do not underestimate the value of having a tourniquet or two on hand. They are relatively cheap to purchase and easy to apply. My church is small, and there is no budget to pay for security. So, I supplied my team with tourniquets and taught them how to use them. It is as simple as that.

Besides a good first-aid kit and tourniquets, your church should have Automated External Defibrillators (AEDs). AEDs are used when people are experiencing sudden cardiac arrest. AEDs can increase the chance of survival by delivering a shock to the person's heart, hopefully returning it to a normal rhythm. The location of these devices needs to be seen by all to eliminate the need to find one during an emergency.

Having one in plain sight shows the congregation and the visitors that the church takes their health and safety seriously. These devices do require training and maintenance, so please reach out to your local fire department or a private, insured company for the training. The checking of the AED batteries should be included on the checklist each month.

Children 3 years of age and under are highly vulnerable to choking hazards. When a child begins to choke, whether it be from food, a toy, or even from a popped balloon, the response time, combined with a proper application of life-saving techniques, is critical. Another needed item to have on hand is a portable anti-choking device. These are based on the premise of dislodging an obstruction in the airway by using suction from the pressure you apply via a small hand-operated pump.

The prices are minimal compared to what the results would be if there were no one around with proper training. This is another item your security team should review to learn how to correctly use the device.

Fire extinguishers

Fire extinguishers are always a good idea and are probably mandated for your facility, no matter what state you reside in. The number of devices and the placement will be based on your local fire codes, building size, and capacity.

Your security team and your staff must understand how to operate a fire extinguisher and what its capabilities are. You may be thinking right now that everyone knows how to operate a fire extinguisher. Maybe. But people will panic during a critical incident or emergency and temporarily forget the basics of operation. Train your security team and your staff. When you invite your local fire department out to visit or to feed them, ask them what types of extinguishers would be best for different areas of the facility. You can augment your fire extinguishers by adding products on the market.

These are usually cheaper and come in small aerosol cans, but be careful. They are usually meant for minor fires but do not have the capability of real extinguishers.

The bottom line is that having first-aid kits, anti-choking devices, tourniquets/trauma kits, AEDs, and proper fire extinguishers can be both comforting and life-saving.

You cannot prepare for every medical issue or episode known to man, but you can provide assistance to some extent until the first responders arrive. Having an adequately trained security team can comfort the congregation and show the level of caring that people desire.

The building is used as an emergency shelter for the public

That is a question only you can answer. What this question does not address is the issue of the homeless population. This question deals with an actual emergency based on natural, crime, or man-made factors, such as gas pipe explosions. There are so many aspects to think about before making that decision. Places of worship that can transform into emergency shelters can greatly assist the community and ease the load of limited resources. Before considering this option, I encourage you to talk to your insurance company, landlord if renting, and the local authorities to determine if this is legal. If you are allowed to proceed, there are many factors to consider before making this noble gesture.

Review the below and determine if you can even handle the workload that will accompany such accommodations.

1. Enough restrooms and supplies

2. Enough open space for people to rest and lie down.

3. The capability to accept pets as well.

4. Kitchens or places to store frozen food.

5. Enough staff and volunteers on hand, 24 hours a day, to assist with providing care.

6. Do you have anything to offer besides a warm place, such as blankets, food, and water?

Other things to consider are increased utility use (if operable), which means an increase in the monthly bill, and hygiene issues if there is an extended timeline based on the emergency. Some will come as families, while others might come by themselves, which means you need to think about the safety of everyone in your facility. Handling the traffic flow could become a problem once people know you are offering a safe place.

Before opening your house of worship to the community during a disaster, you should have some rules or regulations in place. Below are a few suggestions:

1. All rules are enforced.

2. Anyone seeking refuge will be required to fill out a registration form. (If needed, this will help the police locate people who have been reported missing by others.)

3. No alcohol or illegal drugs will be allowed on the premises.

4. Those who are using the facility will be responsible for their prescription drugs and medical directions. Any prescription drug(s) found unattended will be confiscated and returned only to the person whose name appears on the bottle.

5. No firearms will be allowed in the building.

6. Unruly activity will not be allowed and will be subject to immediate removal.

7. No swearing, watching risqué or graphically violent videos, sexual videos, or listening to music that goes against the house of worship's religious beliefs.

If you are serious about adding your establishment to the list of emergency shelters, and depending on how many people you can accommodate, you might have to hire extra security to help keep everyone safe.

Once you decide to become an emergency shelter, review the following links from the Federal Emergency Management Administration (FEMA). The first discusses what is available to help you become a partner with them, and the second provides instructions on how to obtain grants for security. Becoming an emergency shelter should assist you with obtaining some of those grants.

[Faith-Based and Volunteer Partnership Resources | FEMA.gov](#)

[Nonprofit Security Grant Program | FEMA.gov](#)

Feeding and taking care of the residentially challenged

When a place of worship takes on the responsibility of feeding the residentially challenged, it is truly doing God's work and should be commended for such action. My church has an outreach every Wednesday, during which the residentially challenged can stop by, get out of the blazing Las Vegas heat, relax, eat, and hydrate as needed. In the winter, we also provide warm food and warm clothing for them.

However, by doing so, caring for the residentially challenged brings some serious security issues. The first issue is both good and bad. More residentially challenged people will show up when they know food is available at a particular place, location, and time. This can create a logistical nightmare (Do we have enough food?) and can create a safety issue for volunteers and those coming and going.

The good thing is that you are bringing people to a place of love and worship. To effectively handle this, good management might need to be implemented.

Depending on your building, this will come down to the number of entrances and exits you have, and the number of security personnel you incorporate. More importantly, it will come down to being able to communicate crowd control management processes to those seeking food. Clear communication as to expectations and protocols is a must and should be reiterated at every instance. Repetition of expectations and protocols is an opportunity for growth and exercise of proper worship decorum.

Another issue to think about is food safety. Much of this will depend on your local health codes, which you should be fully aware of and know. Also, if you are renting, especially in a strip mall area, you may be limited to the types of food you can and cannot cook. Either way, your staff should always follow safe food handling protocols and only use clean utensils and gloves to avoid transmission of germs and propagation of illnesses and viruses. Food should be handed out by volunteers and not left for people to load up their plates in a buffet style or self-serve. Not everyone thoroughly washes their hands. No one outside of the church staff should be handling food. This is an opportunity for teaching and learning; have clear signs indicating that food will be served by the volunteers to minimize health risks and protect members of the Congregation.

The third concern is having enough volunteers and security on hand to ensure personal safety for everyone. As mentioned previously, being residentially challenged is not a crime, and not every residentially challenged person is a criminal, under the influence of prescribed medication, or illegal drugs. However, the chances do increase of having a residentially challenged person there who may be high or intoxicated. And definitely, the chances are very good that at least one of them will be carrying or have quick access to some type of self-defense weapon. I have had residentially challenged men attempt to walk in with machetes/knives sticking out of their waistbands; one tried to bring in his altered baseball bat that looked like something out of a TV series.

Luckily, not one of them had bad intentions when they brought those items in. They just didn't want to leave those outside for others to steal. Yet, all of them left their items outside when asked to do so. There will never be any justification to allow those types of items/weapons into the church. This is why you have security nearby when serving.

Finally, you need to consider facility security. Just because you invite others into your facilities does not mean they have complete access to all areas.

Lock the doors that need to be locked, have signs or volunteers to help direct people to where you want them to go, and understand this: not all people who come to get fed will be nice. If some are allowed to take a purse or a piece of church equipment, they will.

Overall, feeding the residentially challenged does have its benefits, more for them than for you. And yes, you are meeting the requirement of taking care of the needy and disadvantaged. I encourage you to implement some type of food/clothing program but do it with a thoughtful and comprehensive plan that integrates security.

Chapter Ten
COMMENTS FROM THE SURVEY

Comments and responses from the nationwide survey

The following contains comments from respondents to a survey conducted by Protection With Grace, LLC. While most of the feedback was positive and insightful, some individuals expressed hesitancy about engaging in security discussions. For clarity and ease of review, I've corrected any typos and spelling errors so you can focus solely on the content of the comments.

Comment –

"We meet in a YMCA gym."

I love this response because it highlights the power and impact of a church located in an ideal setting. The physical location draws people in and provides them with the opportunity to share their faith. While the church may not have control over its infrastructure or business hours, it can still implement security measures to protect information, manage financial transactions, and ensure the safety of those entering and leaving the property. This reminds us that the size of the church is not what truly matters; it's the size of its spiritual heart and its positive influence on the community.

Comment –

"Though we don't have a formal, trained security team, our Deacons and IT Team monitor the Church throughout services, and one is retired from the fire department."

Excellent! Most churches do not have formally trained security teams, so please do not worry about that. You understand the need for security and have implemented steps to address it. Monitoring is good, but have you considered actual responses to situations? Have you had scenario-response discussions and seriously asked each other what they would do in situations? These types of conversations tend to build better teamwork and open the door for more options that others may not have thought of.

Comment –

"We are working on expanding policies and procedures, and we have had our church building and grounds reviewed by the local police department and by a security company, both of which have written formal reports."

It is fantastic to make use of local resources. As I have mentioned numerous times in this book, I strongly encourage inviting first responders to your church. This will help create beneficial relationships and open doors for those who may consider attending your church.

I like the idea of having multiple plans. However, it is important to review each plan independently and then compare them side by side. This will help identify overlaps and potentially reveal any issues or protocols that still need to be addressed. Keep in mind that private companies are designed to make a profit.

Comment –

"We don't actually have protocols for natural disasters, but I had to give an answer to that question."

I appreciate your straightforward honesty. Thank you for bringing that question to my attention; I will change it for future surveys.

Many churches do not have protocols for natural disasters, so you are not alone in this. Unfortunately, churches often overlook these topics. Plans do not need to be elaborate or difficult, but they are important in case your buildings are damaged or if a disaster affects your community and you need to shelter people. I recommend reaching out to your local fire department or Emergency Manager for assistance.

Comment –

"We need a security plan."

I fully support having a well-thought-out plan in place, which is just as vital as recruiting volunteers for the security team. As previously highlighted, it is imperative to conduct a comprehensive assessment of security needs, clearly define the roles and responsibilities of the security team, and establish robust communication protocols. It's crucial to understand that the level of detail in these plans should be tailored to the specific requirements of the church. Smaller churches may not need extensive protocols as compared to larger, multi-campus churches. Regardless of the size, it is critical to have a carefully crafted plan in place. Recognizing the necessity of a well-designed plan is praiseworthy, and it should be promptly followed up with appropriate action.

Comment –

"We train on DE-ESCALATION, Mental Health. Service interruption."

I find it valuable to acknowledge the importance of statements like these. Preparing for every possible scenario or problem is indeed an impossible task. Nevertheless, we can equip ourselves with training in basic human behavior and conflict resolution techniques. Developing a plan for managing disruptive individuals, whether it's on-site or during worship, is essential.

Comment –

"I have recently taken a position as head of Security from the person who no longer attends. I had a manual for SOPs (standard operating procedures), but I can't locate it. Would like Guidelines for lockdown inside and outside incidents. Dealing with strangers entering backpacks, the procedure for hostile congregants, etc."

This comment deals with the heart of the responses from the survey and one that sets the tone for this book. It basically covers everything a church should consider when setting up a security plan and team. Having a policy in place, as discussed in Chapter 6, defines the need for protocols. It can make your team better, and it will help keep the church safer. The statement about lockdown procedures will be dependent on your facility. Chapter 9 discusses the facility aspect and how to further keep people safe, including protocols for suspicious or unattended packages, while Chapter 7 reviewed procedures on how to deal with disruptive people.

In an earlier part of this book, the focus was on the importance of ensuring continuous business operations. This strongly emphasizes the need for a well-structured plan to ensure the smooth availability of documents for the succeeding personnel.

Moreover, having trained volunteers in place is vital in maintaining the right course of action in the absence of key team members.

Chapter 8 reviewed properly managing emails and updating passwords, as these actions are imperative. They significantly empower the organization to securely maintain all vital documents and protocols if a leader departs for any reason.

As you step into your new role, it's important to establish procedures that will provide a strong foundation for your eventual successor. As long as you know the laws of your state and community, have buy-in from the leadership established in your church, and do not scare the congregation, you are on the right path to make a difference.

Comment –

"We have gone to a workshop, formed a security committee, hired off-duty officers, and are writing safety and security protocols."

YES! I am thrilled to hear about this! If only I knew who wrote this, I would have loved to follow up with them and write about their experiences for this book. It would be so interesting to hear about their journey and the lessons they've learned. Their experiences could offer great advice to others.

Chapter Eleven
CONCLUSION

As we conclude the principles and practices of church security, we must pause and reflect on the essential lessons learned, the persistent challenges that lie ahead, and the profound moral responsibility we carry as custodians of God's house. Hopefully, the book helps us balance a spirit of community and vigilance, reminding us that the safety of our congregants is an integral aspect of fulfilling our mission of faith, hope, love (cf 1 Corinthians 13:13), and service.

The Evolving Landscape of Threats

This book hopefully revealed an important understanding: the nature of the known and unknown threats that churches face daily. Traditionally, churches have served as peaceful havens and places of community. However, this sense of safety has been challenged by an increase in various forms of violence, both internal and external. Incidents like active shooter situations, terrorism, cyberattacks, domestic violence, and vandalism have become realities that church leaders must consider. While most church services occur without issues, remaining conscious of these potential threats is important.

Churches must be prepared for the worst while still embodying the values of hospitality, grace, and welcoming the neighbor and the stranger (cf. Leviticus 19:18, Matthew 25:31-40, Romans 12:13, Hebrews 13:2).

A robust security plan is no longer optional—it is a necessary investment in the health and vitality of the church community. We must acknowledge that churches are sacred spaces and must also be secure from those who would cause harm. Returning to the anonymous statement I mentioned earlier, *"We don't have security because we trust in the Lord,"* is not sound practice. Yes, we trust in the Lord, but we also take measures to ensure the safety of others.

Comprehensive Security Planning
One of the central themes of this book has been the importance of comprehensive security planning. This does not simply mean installing surveillance cameras or hiring security personnel, but creating an integrated and well-rounded strategy that involves every aspect of church life. The best way to accomplish this is to include your congregation. An experienced security plan should cover several key areas:

Physical Security: The physical layout of the church plays a significant role in its security. Well-placed lighting, controlled access points, visible security personnel, and even the consideration of escape routes can make a substantial difference in an emergency. Churches must also consider security measures for parking lots and adjoining properties, which are often vulnerable to criminal activity.

Technological Security: A comprehensive church security plan must include essential components such as surveillance, alarm, and emergency notification systems. Surveillance cameras can monitor the interior and exterior of the church, providing real-time footage that can deter potential threats and improve response times in case of an incident. Alarm systems can alert authorities and church staff to unauthorized entry or emergency situations, ensuring a quick reaction to any breaches in security.

Moreover, emergency notification systems are crucial for communicating alerts to congregants and staff during critical situations, such as active threats or natural disasters.

These systems can include text alerts, public address announcements, and digital signage to ensure everyone is promptly informed.

In addition, access control systems play a significant role in regulating who is allowed to enter and exit the church premises. These systems can include keycard readers, biometric scanners, or keypad entry, allowing only authorized individuals, such as staff members or volunteers, to access certain areas. This enhances security and helps create a safer environment for worshippers by ensuring that only those with good intentions can enter the church. By integrating these technologies, churches can establish a secure and welcoming atmosphere for their congregations.

Cybersecurity: The rise of online giving, digital church events, and other technologically driven ministries has made churches susceptible to cyber threats. Ensuring that sensitive data, such as financial records and personal information of church members, is protected from hackers is crucial. Regular audits of cybersecurity practices and implementing firewalls, encryption, and secure payment methods can help mitigate this risk.

Question—Are you still allowing employees to use personal email addresses for church-related functions? If the answer is yes, please re-read that section, as you are setting yourself up for failure, loss of trust if information leaves the church, and potential lawsuits.

Emergency Response Plans: A vital part of church security is the ability to respond swiftly and effectively to emergencies, whether medical, natural disasters, or acts of violence. Churches must have clear and well-practiced emergency response plans, which should be communicated to staff, volunteers, and the congregation.

Standard practice should be first aid training, fire drills, and active shooter response protocols. Collaboration with local law enforcement and emergency services to develop these plans is important for preparedness.

Invite those first responders out to discuss safety issues, enjoy them, build relationships, and invite them to Services and functions. Seriously, reach out to your local first responders and invite them to events and meals.

Training and Awareness: An informed congregation and trained staff are some of a church's most significant assets in ensuring safety. Whether it's training greeters to spot suspicious behavior, encouraging Church members to report unusual activity, or implementing de-escalation training for ministry leaders, the involvement of the entire congregation in security efforts is paramount. The best defense against potential threats often lies in the attentiveness and vigilance of those present.

Balancing Safety with Hospitality

A central challenge churches face when implementing security measures is the delicate balance between safety and hospitality. Churches have historically been places of welcome for all, and ensuring that the safety measures put in place do not hinder the church's open, inviting nature is crucial. It is essential that security procedures do not inadvertently create barriers that deter people from attending services or events. As I wrote earlier, the best security is one that people do not see.

While it is tempting to think that more security equals less openness, the opposite is true. Churches that demonstrate a clear and well-communicated security plan actually make it easier for members to feel safe, thus enhancing their ability to participate freely in worship and fellowship.

For instance, establishing a visible security presence can comfort parishioners, helping them feel safe while maintaining an inviting atmosphere.

By employing clear and informative signage to outline specific policies, such as bag checks and designated entry points, a church can promote transparency and trust within the community.

This thoughtful approach addresses security concerns and creates a welcoming environment where everyone feels at ease. Ultimately, a church's dedication to safeguarding its congregation sends a powerful message: each individual is valued, and their safety is of the utmost importance.

The Role of Church Leadership in Security

The responsibility for church security falls heavily on the church's leadership. Church leaders must set the tone by recognizing that security is not just a concern for the ushers or designated security teams but a shared responsibility across the congregation. Church leaders must proactively initiate security discussions, collaborate with experts, and allocate the necessary resources to ensure the church is secure.

Moreover, spiritual leadership must address the moral aspects of church security. Churches must avoid fostering fear or paranoia, which goes against the Christian call to live in peace and trust in God's protection. Instead, church leadership should model the principles of love and responsibility. Churches can create environments where members feel empowered to participate in security efforts without compromising their faith in God's care and provision. The ultimate goal is not to turn the church into a fortress but to foster an atmosphere of trust, safety, and openness.

The Future of Church Security

The objective of Church security extends beyond merely protecting structures or individuals; it aims to ensure that the church remains a sanctuary where individuals can engage with God without apprehension. Churches must facilitate meaningful discussions regarding safety, hospitality, and their distinctive role within society. Only through collective effort, wisdom, and prayerful discernment can Churches be adequately equipped to meet present and future challenges.

Church security surpasses mere preventative measures; it encompasses cultivating a culture of awareness, responsibility, and care. The journey toward establishing safe and secure worship environments persists. Church leaders and members are urged to remain vigilant and take a proactive approach, ensuring that God's house stays a sanctuary of peace and joy for everyone. With careful planning, compassionate leadership, and divine grace, Churches will continue to thrive, and the sacred act of worship will persist, free from fear or danger.

If you feel overwhelmed about organizing a dedicated security team, I encourage you to pray with and for your leaders and members. Remembering 1 Peter 4:8-9 can provide inspiration and clarity as you move forward in protecting your community.

> *"Above all, love each other deeply because love covers over a multitude of sins. Offer hospitality to one another without grumbling."*

Let's operate with faith and courage, assured that God accompanies us at every juncture, guiding us to uphold the sanctity of our sacred spaces in safety, warmth, and steadfastness in His love.

ABOUT THE AUTHOR

Rich is a 25-year veteran of the Las Vegas Metropolitan Police Department. He retired in 2018 as a Police Captain and Commander of the Honor Guard. He spent time in Patrol, Traffic, Academy Staff, Range Sergeant, and Internal Affairs Lieutenant. He oversaw two patrol bureaus as a Captain and led the Support Operations Bureau when he retired. He is the recipient of the **Unit Meritorious Award,** the **Unit Exemplary Award,** the **Unit Valorous Conduct Award,** and the **1 October Award.** Other police departments have recognized him for his work with Honor Guard ceremonies. In 2017, he received the *Heart of Courage Award* from Liberty Baptist Church for his community service. Rich worked for one year as the Police Chief for the Moapa Police Department before finally retiring from Law Enforcement.

He recently stepped down as the Director of Ceremonies for the Nevada Law Enforcement Officers Memorial, a position he had held for 10 years.

Rich holds a Master of Public Administration from Troy University and a Bachelor of Criminal Justice from Providence University (formerly College of Great Falls). He is a graduate of Northwestern University's Center for Public Safety Police Staff and Command and a United States Marine Corps veteran.

He is currently an Adjunct Instructor at the College of Southern Nevada, the owner of Protection With Grace, LLC, and serves at his church as both a leader and the Director of Security

Rich has been married to Kim for 34 years and has two children, both of whom are married to wonderful people. When not working, he enjoys spending time with his family and watching his grandchildren grow up.

www.ingramcontent.com/pod-product-compliance
Lightning Source LLC
Chambersburg PA
CBHW070147100426
42743CB00013B/2840